The World of Roses

The World *of* Roses

A practical handbook on the use
of the rose from ancient
to modern times

SONNI BONE and BETTY CLARK

FLICKERS MEDIA PRODUCTIONS

1990

CANADIAN CATALOGUING IN PUBLICATION DATA

Bone, Sonni
      The world of roses

ISBN 0-9694161-0-5

1. Roses – Miscellanea. I. Clark, Betty, 1929–   II. Title
SB411.B65 1990   635.9'33372   C89–091591–1

Illustrations by Marjolein Witteman
Cover by Sherle Raitt

Our research continues. If you would like to share your 'rose' stories, recipes or ideas, please contact the publishers at:

                      THE WORLD of ROSES
                      Flickers Media Productions
                      43 Van Horne Street
                      Penticton, British Columbia
                      Canada V2A 4J9
                      (604)493-5439

Bulk distributor: Sandhill Book Marketing
                      Box 197 – Station A
                      Kelowna, British Columbia
                      Canada V1Y 7N5
                      (604)763-1406

Printed in Canada by: Hignell Printing Ltd.
                      488 Burnell Street
                      Winnipeg, Manitoba, R3G 2B4

To our husbands, Don and Phil,
for their constant support through
rose garden and briar patch.

"A rose is a rose is a rose............."
GERTRUDE STEIN

THE AUTHORS

Sonni Bone has spent years researching, growing and smelling roses. She manufactures her own natural cosmetic line, using roses as a main ingredient in many of her recipes. She is a newspaper and TV personality, hosting her own cable TV show. She is married to orchardist Don Godfrey, with whom she shares a love of the earth. It was their shared interest in the growing of roses that brought them together. Don still shows his affection with a weekly gift of fresh red roses. Sonni and Don have six children.

Betty Clark is a marketing agent and video consultant. Her interest in all things beautiful, especially the rose, led her to making a TV video on roses with partner Sonni. That in turn led to the book on roses. Betty is married to visual artist, Phil, whose work she promotes all over the world. They share a love of literature, old movies and life on the fringe of civilization. The Clarks have two boys.

Both authors are Canadian and reside in the Okanagan Valley, British Columbia—great rose-growing country! The Okanagan with its beautiful flowers, blossoms, fruits, herbs and grasses has all the attributes of Grasse, France, the perfume capital of the world. Down one road you may encounter the sweet smell of roses, down another the punguent smell of sage.

Table of Contents

Introduction

Searching through the literature on roses, we could not find a 'recipe book' of ways to use roses.

One book might contain a recipe for perfume, another a recipe for jam, another a suggestion for arranging roses. But we wanted a comprehensive collection where roses could become a part of our everyday living and loving. This book, therefore, brings together in one volume, the information we have collected.

Our book is brimming with dozens of modern ways to use roses—in your bath, on your face, at your dinner table, in your bed, in your language and music, and in your sick room.

Here we are offering you a rose garden of ideas, many of them based on Roman days when roses garlanded the heads of the worthy Romans, floated in their wine and acted as a medicine when they were ill. They ate rose honey and rose puddings, drank rose wine. Burnt roses were used as mascara and fresh roses were used as an aphrodisiac. At one of Nero's celebrations, four million sesterces' (about $100,000) worth of roses paved the city with their sweetness.

We enjoyed compiling this book and we hope because it is so easy to use, that you too will enjoy living with every room a rose.

"One should make a decision," says Ippolito Pizzetti in his 'Comprehensive Flowers; A Guide for Your Garden', "to have nothing whatever to do with roses that do not have a rose-like fragrance."

1

Growing Roses

Because of their fragrance and beauty, over the centuries roses have been the most popular plant on earth. During the peak of the Roman Empire rose cultivation reached its zenith. Methods were developed to force roses to bloom during the winter by growing them in green houses or irrigating the plants with warm water.

Today, rose fanciers have become the largest organized group of flower growers in North America. Their intense interest leads to an exchange of rose varieties and cultural information with other enthusiasts throughout the world.

As well, florists sell more roses than all other flowers and in the winter, more than all the rest put together.

But have they lost their Fragrance? Although they remain the Queen of Flowers, a common complaint one hears today is that modern roses are losing their fragrance due to the hybridizers' emphasis on form, color and repeat-flowering qualities. This may be true of a number, but many varieties carry as much fragrance as old-fashioned roses.

There is a difference in the fragrance of old and new. Each type of ancient European rose had its distinctive and beloved scent—damask, gallica, musk, alba, scentifolia, and so on—whereas the scent of modern roses has become mixed by an infusion of many strains.

Heavenly Scents The fragrance of any rose is dictated mostly by the compound geraniol. Also there are eight or nine other substances present to give the rose a more distinct fragrance, determined by the proportion of these substances in a particular variety.

These substances are chemically allied to substances present in fruits. Thus we recognize lemon, apple, apricot, orange or even the banana in the 'fruity' fragrance of many roses. Henry Ford has a lemon-like fragrance while Chantre smells like ripe apricots. *R. soulieana*, a massive bush smothered in tiny white flowers, smells exactly like ripe bananas.

R. andersonii a replica of the wild rose, but deeper pink with larger flowers has a pronounced raspberry perfume. The blue rose, Sterling Silver, and the pink rose, Silver Lining, both have a scent reminiscent of a soft face cream.

The Royal National Rose Society chose Silver Lining as a gift to Queen Elizabeth II to commemorate the birth of Prince Andrew. Now growing in Buckingham Palace gardens, beneath her majesty's window, is a bed of more than 100 plants of this lovely rose.

A rose with a strong spice scent is Carmen Talon, a fine dark red rose. Two roses with a violet perfume are Elsa Arnot, with deep pink and creamy-yellow flowers and the pale pink, Dr. Debat. The florabunda, Elizabeth of Glamis, has a delicious cinnamon scent while the silvery-pink Conrad Meyer (great for growing up a pillar) has a strong clove scent. *R. moscha*, a white musk rose has an intense musk perfume.

As you can see the perfumes of roses are almost as varied as the size and form of the blooms.

Geneology   All ancient roses and their descendants are, in botanical terms, members of a single group or genus, Rosa, that is a part of a much larger family of shrubs, herbs and trees known as Rosaceae. The roses' closest relatives include strawberries, raspberries and hawthorne, peach, almond, apple and apricot.

1. **Species Rose**s: are found growing in the wild. In the genus Rosa there are over 150 species from which all other roses are descended. Shrub roses are close relatives of species roses which have been improved by hybridizers for garden culture. The line that divides them is very narrow.

2. **Old Garden Roses**: are rose varieties and cultivars (the different versions of species are called varieties. The varieties developed by hybridizers are called cultivars).

   Old Garden Roses are clearly identifiable before 1867 with a specific group of roses. The American Rose Society established the 1867 date to commemorate the debut of what was considered the first hybrid tea rose, 'La France'. It turned up by chance in the gardens of rose breeder J.B. Guillot, near Lyons, France, a sweet, silvery pink believed to be a descendent of the bright pink 'Madame Victor Verdier' and the creamy white, 'Madame Bravy'. But no one knows for sure.

3. **The Modern Roses**: are all rose groups introduced after 1867. Two different roses can be combined to produce a rose that has characteristics of both parents but an identity of its own. In the hybridization process, the pollen of one fertilizes the other—the 'child' is a hybrid. This happens frequently in nature, but hybridizers have developed it into an intricate art form.

There are five main groups of Modern roses: the hybrid teas, polyanthas, floribundas, grandifloras and miniatures.

Hybrid Teas, the most widely grown rose in the world today, are a result of breeding and inter-breeding between hybrid perpetuals and tea roses. Blooming prolifically from early summer until the first frost, their long narrow buds open into delicate blossoms. The blossoms, usually double and fragrant, are born singly on straight, tensile stems. Height is from 2 1/2 to 3 1/2 feet, though some varieties reach 6 feet. There are a wide range of colors.

Polyanthas are a cross between the Oriental Rosa multiflora and hybrid teas. Low-growing (up to 2 feet) they are ideal for massed planting and low hedges. They produce a great quantity of small flowers in clusters from late spring through fall and are much hardier than hybrid teas.

Floribunda have eclipsed polyanthas in popularity. Low-growing (2 to 3 feet) and exuberant, they bloom continuously from late spring through autumn. The flowers are borne in clusters and colors cover the whole range of the hybrid tea.

Grandifloras exploit the best qualities of the hybrid tea and the floribunda. Plants grow 3 to 6 feet and are ideal as background borders. Blooms are usually double without a striking fragrance. The flowers, borne either singly or in clusters, come in a multiplicity of colors.

Miniatures : there are more than 200 varieties ranging in height from 4 to 18 inches (the average about 1 foot). Exceptions are a few climbing roses that, if not supported, sprawl along the ground to a distance of 5 feet. It is even possible to buy miniature tree roses 10 to 14 inches high. Most miniatures bloom continuously from spring to frost producing clusters of 1/2 to 2 inch blossoms in a large variety of colors. They are popular as edgings for beds and borders, as accent plants in small rock gardens and as house plants.

Tree Roses These are not a class of roses by themselves but a distinct garden form. Almost any rose can be made into a tree rose by grafting the selected cultivar onto a sturdy trunk of established root stock. To keep their shape tree roses need a careful but light pruning.

Choosing Your Roses

There are roses for formal and informal plantings, for many landscaping effects including insuring privacy, for keeping the garden bright with color, and for keeping the home stocked with cut flowers.

Seeds, cuttings and buddings can be used to propagate roses. If you choose to use these methods, consult books on growing roses.

The amateur rose grower should stick to nursery stock—especially if the roses are desired for herbal use and not primarily for exhibit or display.

It will be your pleasurable task to choose the roses best adapted to your needs. Though you may be entranced by photographs of roses when going through seed catalogues or rose garden books, some practical considerations should be kept in mind—winter hardiness, disease resistance, ease of maintenance, and plant size.

Some Great Roses There are hundreds of roses to choose from. British hybridizers alone are adding fifty new roses a year and there are test gardens all over North America where roses are being developed. Many are highly scented.

The petals of highly scented roses have, on their surface, tiny perfume glands invisible to the naked eye which may be observed under a powerful microscope. Old cabbage and Damask roses with their thick velvet-like petals produce a stronger fragrance than those which have thin petals. That is why they are used for distillation.

Some roses have fragrant leaves such as Shakespeare's englantine, the sweet briar. Among others are *R. glutinosa* with its strong pine smell and *R. primula* with its heavy incense-like perfume.

The following short list of roses is a suggested starting point for the novice gardener who wants fragrant varieties.

1. **Species Roses**

   Rosa rugosa: 3 1/2 to 4 inch semidouble, carmine color, cinnamon fragrance. Repeat bloom. Upright, 3 to 6 feet. Hardy. Disease-resistant. Hips large. Good for hedges.

2. **Shrub Roses**

   Blanc Double de Coubert: 2 to 3 inch semidouble, white, very fragrant. Glossy foliage. 4 by 5 feet. Disease-resistant. Hardy.

   Constance Spry: 3 1/2 to 5 inch double, pink, strong scent. Mid-summer bloom. Dark foliage, 7 by 7 feet, arching. Good for hedge, fence or pillar.

3. **Old Garden Roses**

   Rosa gallica officinalis: 2 to 3 inch semidouble, red, strong fragrance. Mid-summer bloom. Used in potpourri and attar of roses. Rough and dark foliage. Medium size to 4 feet.

   Rosa damascena semperflorens: 3 1/2 inch double, pink, very fragrant. Useful for potpourri and rose oil. Recurrent in warm climates. Rough, light green foliage. Vigorous bush to 5 feet. Hardy. Also see OLD ROSE section below.

4. **Hybrid Tea Roses**

   Bewitched: 5 inch double, pure pink, spicy, old-fashioned fragrance. Long pointed buds, glossy foliage. Tall, bushy. Disease-resistant. Easy to grow.

   Sutter's Gold: 4 to 5 inch double, golden orange tinged with salmon pink, heavy, fruity fragrance. Good cut. Dark, leathery foliage. Very vigorous spreading 3 to 4 feet tall. Color best in cool weather. Very disease-resistant.

   Chrysler Imperial: 4 1/2 to 5 inch double, crimson red with darker shading, heavy, spicy fragrance. Moderate blooming. Long stems, good cut. Dark green foliage. Upright bush to 4 feet. Needs summer heat to perform well.

5. *Floribundas*

   Angel Face: 4 inch double, mauve-lavender, heavy, old-fashioned fragrance. Good cut. Dark, leathery foliage. Compact, bushy to 2 feet. Disease-resistant.

   Spartan: 3 to 3 1/2 inch double, orange-red to reddish-coral, heavy fragrance. Free-blooming. Dark, glossy foliage. Vigorous grower to 3 feet. Disease-resistant.

6. *Grandiflora*

   Queen Elizabeth: 3 1/2 to 4 inch double, carmine rose and pale pink, moderate fragrance. Profuse, continual, long-lasting blooms. Excellent cut. Dark, glossy foliage. Very vigorous 4 to 6 feet. Very hardy. Very disease-resistant. A classic.

7. *Climbers*

   America: 4 to 5 inch double, coral pink, spicy, carnation-like fragrance. Hybrid tea-like flowers. Profuse bloomer all season. Dark, leathery foliage. Moderately tall. Disease-resistant, hardy. Easy to grow. Good for pillars.

   Climbing Crimson Glory: 3 to 4 inch double, deep crimson with purple shadings, rich fragrance. Good cut. Leathery foliage. Vigorous grower to 10 feet. Quite hardy.

   Don Juan: 4 to 5 inch double, dark red, heavy fragrance. Profuse, long-lasting flowers throughout season. Good cut. Dark, leathery foliage. Vigorous, upright grower to 8 feet. Disease-resistant. Fairly hardy.

8. *Miniature Roses*

   Beauty Secret: 1 to 1 1/2 inches semidouble, cardinal red, very fragrant. Hybrid tea-like buds. Abundant bloom. Good cut. Glossy, leathery foliage. 8 to 10 inches. Very hardy. Good in semi-shade.

   Cinderella: 3/4 to 1 inch double, white with pale pink edging, spicy fragrance. Prolific. Good cut. Glossy foliage. 12 to 15 inches. Thornless. Disease-resistant. Easy to grow. Excellent in pots.

   Sweet Fairy: 3/4 to 1 inch double, apple blossom pink, strong fragrance. Blooms profusely. 6 to 8 inches.

1988 Rose of the Year   The Royal National Rose Society's choice for the Rose of the Year Award (1988) went to the beautiful Dwarf Cluster Flowered (patio) rose 'Sweet Dream' (Fryminicot). This sweetly scented disease-resistant rose has masses of medium sized, double peachy apricot blooms which are non-fading and unaffected by rain. It is neat, compact, 16 to 20 inches high with dense, glossy foliage and is great as a cut flower.

Old Roses The nostalgic gardener who wants to grow a fragrant rose or two from the past, must replace visions of the hybrid teas with their long, narrow buds opening on long stems, with a vision of roses that are rounder, flatter, and more loosely made.

Favorites of the Queen Mother, who loves old-fashioned roses, are the moss rose, 'William Lobb', the deep reddish-purple Gallica rose, 'Tuscany Superb' and the Rosa rugosa 'Blanc Double de Coubert'.

Patrick Lima in 'The Harrowsmith Illustrated Book of Herbs' says "Modern roses are to old roses what Vogue models, all bone structure and paint, are to Rubens female figures—plump, pink and glowing from a bath, scented no doubt with rosewater". Lima's favorite old rose is Rosa Mundi (*R. gallica versicolor*). It is derived from *R. gallica* as is the Apothecary rose, *R. gallica officinalis*.

Rosa Mundi flowers are loosely semi-double, several rows of petals surrounding a central mass of golden stamens. Says Lima, the flower is "unlike any other rose I know, the petals are variously striped crimson, pink and white. The fragrance is heady."

Also among Lima's favorite old roses growing at Larkwhistle, an extraordinary garden near Miller Lake, Ontario, where he lives, is 'Konigin von Danemark' (Queen of Denmark—an alba hybrid growing four feet tall). This rose with 2 1/2 to 4 inch double blooms is pure pink, highly fragrant and has blue-green foliage. It spreads to seven feet.

Loved too, for their fragrance and old-fashioned beauty, are varieties of *R. scentifolia*, the 100-leaved or cabbage rose, so often depicted in the floral art of Dutch masters (see VISUAL ARTS section). The blooms of this rose and the Provence rose have a rich perfume as do their offspring, the moss roses, whose buds are covered in hairs to give them the appearance of being covered in moss.

In the book 'The Old Shrub Roses' by Graham Stuart Thomas, (published by Charles T. Branford, Boston) there is a section on the Apothecary's or Rose of Provins. It was in the little French town of Provins, in the 13th century that the local apothecaries discovered a red rose that could be reduced to powder and still retain its fragrance (not to be confused with the rose of Provence, *R. centifolia*, the Cabbage rose).

These old-fashioned roses are wonderful candidates for your herb garden. Colorful, fragrant, free-flowering and trouble free, some of these bushes also give crops of large hips.

Planting Your Roses

Roses love to be pampered so if you plant them to suit their personalities, they will offer optimum performance.

They will perform best in fairly heavy clay loam that has been dug deeply and enriched with organic matter.

They also need a well drained location that sunshine reaches for at least half a day. Water accumulating at root level can literally drown a rose; the roots need air as well as moisture.

Roses want their own space. No poachers please. They are extremely susceptible to root competition from other plants especially tree roots. These should be sealed off from the rose bed by metal underground shields of anodized aluminum or galvanized metal sheeting. Roses cannot compete with many perennials. To grow outstanding roses, plant them in a well prepared bed by themselves.

They prefer their beds dug 1 1/2 to 2 feet deep. Remove the soil and mix with organic matter and additives. (Roses prefer a pH of 6.5 to 6.8 but they will grow in soils from a pH of 6.0 to 7.5). Fill the bed just slightly lower than the adjacent lawn so that it will hold water when flooded.

Mixing a phosphorous compound into the soil helps them to grow strong roots.

Plant the roses one foot from the edge of the bed and 30 inches or more apart depending on their eventual size. They do not like crowding— because their foliage is susceptible to mildew and they need sun. Nor do they like to be planted in hollows and can die from the cold air that accumulates there.

For budded roses, heap the soil in the middle of the hole and arrange roots on either side of the hump, making sure they do not cross. Do not crowd the roots in the hole. Set the collar (the point of the graft) two inches beneath the soil surface and pack soil around it.

For potted or packaged roses, the holes need not be much larger than the containers. Plant as soon as the spring weather has settled. Fill the hole with water. Insert the plant a little deeper than it stood in the pot and tamp firmly around it.

Climbing roses need support but otherwise are planted in the same way. Do not plant too close to porches or you may have slugs. Climbing roses are divided into two groups, those with large flowers which have rigid thick canes, and ramblers which have very long (10 to 20 feet) thinner flexible canes. Both groups, given something to 'lean on', will grow with abandon.

HINT: For an inexpensive support for roses, cut old pantyhose into strips. The strips are firm, pliable and soft, do not damage the rose buds or stems and become almost invisible.

Pruning and Mulching Roses are pruned to shape the plant, reduce care, and increase bloom size. Prune roses in late winter or early spring. Keep inside branches cut so air can circulate through the bush.

Old roses do not like to be tamed. They prefer to grow naturally atangle. Spring pruning is necessary but should be restrained. Cut the willowy canes by about one third and remove any weak twiggy growth. After three or four seasons, some of the crowded canes can be cut to ground level to make room for new growth.

Roses hate weeds so cultivate them frequently, but only one to one-and-a-half inches deep to eliminate weeds and prevent hard crusts from forming. Deep cultivation can destroy feeder roots.

In the spring, top dress with compost, manure or compost tea.

Manure and mulch should also be applied in the fall. Remove mulch in the spring. Also mulch in dry weather. Keep soil moist, but not wet, watering heavily but not more than once a week.

In a herb bed, old fashioned roses are one of the plants that profit most from mulch. They can be mulched heavily with leaf mold, straw, or rough compost (peat moss is a poor mulch because it dries out to an unyielding crust), either in the fall, when a layer of mulch is good winter protection, or in early summer when the ground has warmed and plants have grown out of reach of slugs.

Black plastic or shredded newspaper can also be used as mulch for roses. If desired, cover the plastic or paper with more attractive materials. Punch holes in plastic for water penetration.

Fertilizers Most roses need regular application of fertilizer to achieve their optimum growth and flower production. Dry fertilizers are worked into the ground and spread to the roots by watering. Liquid fertilizers are added to water and applied to the roots.

Most rose gardeners rely on one 'complete' dry fertilizer, supplemented by a liquid fertilizer. However, others 'swear by' their own proven methods such as the following two:

1. Dig a one inch trench close around rose bush. Add one box of 12 aspirins to a gallon of water. Fill trench with aspirin water. If you do this every three weeks, this is all the fertilizer your roses will need, says one rose expert.
2. Another expert says try fish heads. Dig down carefully among the roots 5 or 6 inches. Put in a medium fish head and cover well. Water abundantly. For large bushes and climbers, use two heads, one on either side of the plant. The fish heads will supply all the nutrients the roses need, lasting for an entire season and possibly into a second.

Weekly Watering Keep soil moist but not wet. Water heavily but not more than once a week. Water roses at ground level. Overhead watering is conducive to the growth of mildew.

Pests Roses are susceptible to black spot, mildew, canker and rust. Rose pests include aphids, leafhoppers, thrips, Japanese beetles, spider mites, rose bugs and rose slugs.

Many beginners are puzzled by the many rose diseases and afflictions. 'Cures' is a word to forget—the logical word is 'prevention'. Spray before diseases appear and at the manufacturers' recommended dosage. It is also worth remembering that black spot attacks the mature and (lower) leaves first and mildew starts on the new immature growth that spores over-winter in the beds if so allowed.

Many gardeners use soapy dishwater as a wash to clean the leaves and to eliminate aphids and other bugs.

Labels Remove wire-attached name tags from roses (the wire can cut growing roses) and attach to a stake near your plant. Also make a diagram of your rose garden and write names of roses, color, fragrance, date planted, and any other pertinent details.

More Knowledge for Novices Rose beds can be any size or shape but usually the amount of space available will determine the layout. Whatever shape you decide on, do not make it too big. It is best to keep the bed to four feet or less across (make it as long as you like). Roses do not like their soil trampled down, so with this four foot width of bed you will be able to reach all the roses without having to put more than one foot down in the bed.

If you have set your heart on a large circular bed, divide it into segments with paths running into the centre. You could put a variety of rose in each segment and a standard rose in the centre to give height. Large square beds can also be divided into smaller beds by paths.

Cluster Flowered varieties will give greater continuity of bloom, and usually will stand up to rough weather better than Large Flowered roses. With many of the latter there may be several weeks pause between each flush of flowers. It is best not to try to plant Cluster Flowered and Large Flowered varieties in the same bed as their habit of growth is different.

It is also best not to mix your varieties. There can be up to three weeks difference between the flowering peak of one flowered rose and another (one Cluster Flowered rose and another) so that while mixing the varieties will spread the period of bloom, at times the overall effect will be patchy.

There may be considerable height variations too, so properly plan your bed with the taller roses at the back or in the centre. (A 6 foot rose and a 2 foot rose are hardly ideal companions in a small bed!) Pick those of more or less uniform height and plant them in not less than five bushes of one variety. Make sure, of course, that the colors are harmonious.

If the bed is large you can use tall, leggy varieties. Otherwise choose compact and bushy roses which cover the ground well. For a bed which borders on a path, do not select varieties that sprawl.

Roses which are very lax or which branch out widely take up more room than others; you will need fewer of them. By far the best way to judge how close to plant roses is to see your chosen varieties growing in a garden before you buy them. Visit your municipal gardens; when on holidays take in some of the famous ones. Also by joining your local garden club you may get to see private gardens.

Allowing 30 inches between plants suits the majority of bedding roses. This distance prevents the roots of one rose robbing nourishment from its neighbors. It allows for proper circulation and efficient weeding, spraying and mulching.

The most attractive surrounding for rose beds is grass although paving stones or gravel can be used. Gravel must be laid on a proper foundation or it will gradually vanish into the earth.

Common sense means planning your rose bed on paper first, then pegging out the bed. Try to visualize the bed in years ahead when the bushes have reached their various potentials. Remember, with roses, unlike many other garden plants, that you are planting a 'promise'.

Growing Miniature Roses Indoors

Miniature roses (or 'minis') because of their size can be grown indoors in containers. They grow 6 to 18 inches tall with most averaging around 12 inches. It is believed they are derived from a Chinese native, *Rosa chinensis minima*, introduced to the west in the early 1900's. Today there are hundreds of varieties.

If all you want to do is put pots of miniature roses on the sideboard and water them occasionally, then keep the plant indoors for as short a time as possible.

However, if you want year round results, it is necessary to provide fluorescent lighting and a humid atmosphere around the roses. Then they will bloom year round except for about two months. If you pot them at various times, you can have continual bloom.

Pebble Tray Method Using this method you can have bloom by early spring and produce regular flowering until early autumn. In the autumn transfer the pots outdoors and bring them in again by the middle of December. To protect from frost while outside, place them along a wall of a heated room and cover them with straw.

Two weeks before placing them in the house, prune to half their height and stand them in an unheated room. Avoid temperatures above 70°F.

Some growers of miniature roses suggest an annual eight week rest for the roses during the hottest summer months. Place the plants in the vegetable crisper of the refrigerator. After the forced dormancy, cut the plant back to one half its size and resume normal care.

Pebble Tray Planting Choose waterproof trays about 2 inches deep. Put in one layer of gravel. Keep the bottom of this layer wet at all times, but the water level must be kept below the top of the gravel. Routine washing of foliage in the sink will help add moisture.

Plant the miniatures in 4 to 8 inch pots using equal parts of sterilized garden soil, peat moss (or other organic humus), and coarse sand (or pearlite).

Place the tray with pots of roses in a south-facing window. Screen from the midday sun in summer. At nights, in spring and autumn, move the pots under fluorescent light fixtures that provide 20 watts of light per square foot. Keep the light source 10 to 12 inches above the tops of the roses. Set the lights on a timer to establish your routine of 16 to 18 hours per day.

Water liberally, allowing the pots to dry out slightly between waterings. Yellow leaves indicate inadequate drainage or too much water. Feed monthly with a house plant fertilizer. Mist leaves frequently with a hand sprayer. Keep a careful watch for red spider mite.

Growing Miniatures Outdoors

Trough Method Miniature roses can be grown in a trough made from concrete. But it must be deep enough (at least 15 inches) to provide the roots with cool, moist conditions. Try an old bathtub. To be long-lived the roses must never be allowed to suffer from lack of moisture during summer.

For the roses to be successful, place trough in a sunny position, on a veranda, terrace or in a courtyard. Do not put where moisture from trees or from the eaves of a house drips on the plants. Placed near a window, the trough garden will bring great pleasure to anyone confined to the house.

Because troughs are extremely heavy, they should be put in a permanent position before preparing them for the plants. The miniature roses should be planted from small pots. This means you could plant them at any time of the year, weather permitting. The roses should be planted in groups of two or three, 4 to 5 inches apart.

Some suitable roses are: Baby Crimson, Bo-peep, *R. roulettii*, Elf, Sweet Fairy, Mon Petite, Pixie and Humpty Dumpty. All grow no more than 6 inches tall. Always keep the compost comfortably moist and to prevent splashing, cover the surface with wood chips.

Requiring a minimum of attention, the trough garden is an ideal way to enjoy roses outdoors.

2 Dining Table & Household Decor

Fortunatus, Bishop of Poitiers in the 6th century, describes a banquet given by a royal lady who had established a nunnery near Poitiers. At this banquet he says that the floor was strewn "with so many flowers that one seemed to be walking in an enameled meadow" and "the dishes (were) wreathed, while garlands hung on the refectory walls in the manner of the Ancients. .... As for the table, it offered more roses than an entire field. The dishes reposed directly upon the roses. Instead of a linen cloth one had preferred to cover the table with something agreeable and fragrant."

In Paris in the 16th century, shops advertised garlands of roses to be given to banquet guests.

In the 17th century, head stewards looped garlands around the banquet hall or twisted them around the columns. Often they placed them against the tablecloth or swung them from one basket of flowers to another down the entire length of the table.

The 18th century vogue for garlands, almost an obsession, was prevalent not only in France but also all over Europe. Their fashion was adopted even in Russia in the 1730's by the Empress Anne, who, Christopher Marsden says, dined under a pavilion of green silk supported by voluted pillars with wreaths of fresh flowers twisted around them.

In 'Palmyra of the North', Marsden describes a party which took place in Russia during the reign of Empress Anne. The tables were covered with moss with flowers stuck in as if they were growing. The guests sat on benches also made to look like turf.

More Rosy Dinners   Often small intimate suppers were given to celebrate a birthday or extol a very special person's achievement in the arts. At these suppers a candelabra or a plaster cherub was adorned with a garland of roses or a simple wreath was fashioned to surround a basket of roses.

On one occasion at Versailles, a strip of flowers which went the length of the table was changed with each course.

Although today we don't usually scatter flowers on the table in medieval fashion, an independent and imaginative hostess might find it amusing to ignore convention and scatter roses for both a calculated effect and conversation value.

Or, she might decorate a long table bearing openwork baskets of glass filled with roses, with a garland of roses binding one basket with another. Then to add to the brilliance, she could intersperse candlesticks on either side of the baskets.

Not the Real Thing   By the 18th century, artificial flowers were the rage all over Europe. Indeed at this time real flowers were regarded as poor substitutes for those of porcelain or silk, particularly when used on the table.

Vases were placed on brackets or over doorways, and many garlands, now slender and delicate (and often artificial), swung gaily from point to point. We can make good use of wall vases today with space so limited in our smaller houses and apartments.

In Rennaisance paintings, flowers are often shown placed about a room where people are dining. Sometimes roses are caught up behind a painted coat of arms on the wall, or vases of roses are placed on a high mantel or the projection of a cornice. In his 'Last Supper' Ghirlandaio painted two lovely vases of flowers on a ledge high over the scene.

Rose Bowls   In the first decade of this century every North American family had a rose bowl—a round glass vase with a fairly small opening. Some were plain, more were ornate. Some were of clear glass shaped like a goldfish bowl, others were heavier pressed or cut glass with a diamond pattern. Some were decorated with delicate gold or silver filigree patterns, others were inset with glass gems. On occasion, some were fashioned completely from silver. (A silver rose bowl with a frog would make a very special 25th anniversary gift for a rose lover.)

'March' Stand The Victorian epergne was very popular in the 19th century, as was the 'March' stand which made a great sensation at a London flower show. The stand consists of two flat, shallow receptacles fastened at top and bottom to a tall slender glass rod.

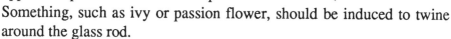

If you make one, the roses in the large container at the base should be short stemmed and impaled in sand or clay. In the upper receptacle the roses droop or trail. Something, such as ivy or passion flower, should be induced to twine around the glass rod.

The stand carries the upper roses above eye level and its slender supporting rod does not obscure the view of guests sitting at a dining table.

The Table in Winter The idea of using flowering plants indoors in winter to give a party a festive air was greatly fostered by the Victorians who filled their conservatories, hallways and bay windows with roses and other exotic plants.

And of Course in the Food A delightfully casual use of fresh flowers fashionable in the 18th century was as a garnish for supper dishes. This tradition of edible flowers also goes deep into European cuisine.

Fresh flowers heighten the visual presentation and enhance the fragrance of many dishes. The petals, with their fragrant, delicate, slightly sweet smell and flavor, are lovely in soups and salads, main dishes, jams, sorbets, syrup and ice cream (see FOOD section).

Bouquets to Eat It is customary in parts of the Middle East to pass a 'bouquet' of fresh herb sprigs to eat along with the meal. You can make an edible herb bouquet, by collecting herbs available from your garden or market—parsley, watercress, chives, cress, dill, coriander, green onions, tarragon, mint. Wash, chill, and arrange the sprigs in a bowl. Add a few edible roses for flavor and color.

In Italy sprigs of fresh basil are served in little individual vases or vials of water to keep the herb fresh. You might add a fresh rose.

A 'garden of herbs' can also be placed on the table. Set several small pots of herbs including a miniature rose in a wicker tray, a large dish, or a wooden flat. This 'garden' can be carried from windowsill to table. For freshness and crispness be sure to wash each individual pot under running water about two hours before dinner and allow to drain.

Give each guest a small pair of scissors along with their tableware and let them clip sprigs of fresh herbs to add to salads, soups, etc.

Finger Bowls In the middle ages, rosewater was used for hand washing at the table. For a modern touch use rosewater in finger bowls and float rose petals in it.

Cutting Roses for the Table

The best times to cut roses from your garden are in the late afternoon, at dusk, or in the early morning when the air is still cool. Choose roses that are just opening or are opened half way. Flowers in full bloom will not last long.

Use sharp shears or a knife to make a 45° angle cut just above a five leaflet leaf. New growth will originate from the base of the leaf. Carry a bucket of tepid water and plunge roses into it. Keep cool until you are ready to arrange them.

If you follow the method given below your roses will look fresher and last days longer.

Arrangements In the book, 'Period Flower Arrangement' by Margaret Fairbanks Marcus (Barrows, 1952), Marcus tells us that the earliest record of flowers arranged 'in a container' in the Western world is a first-century

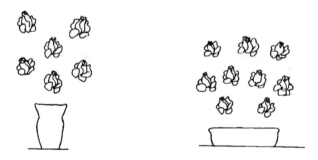

A.D. Roman mosaic, which an accompanying illustration shows as a basket of roses, anemones, pinks and smaller unidentifiable flowers.

Method When arranging roses choose containers that suit the mood of the room or occasion, and relate to the size of the bloom. Clear crystal or glass allow you to view the entire rose; silver reflects its beauty. Tiny teacups and creamers are ideal for miniatures. Wicker baskets are great for casual bouquets.

The arrangement itself is a matter of personal taste—be it formal, casual or simple Oriental.

1. Remove any leaves that might decay below the water level in your vase. Remove thorns.
2. When removing leaves or thorns, do not cut through the bark. Do not scrape the bark.
3. With a sharp knife, give the roses a fresh 45° angle cut an inch off the end of each stem.
4. Place roses in a clean deep vase of warm water (about 120°F). If possible, leave them in a cool room or refrigerator to 'condition' for two to four hours before arranging.
5. You can add a good floral preservative if you desire. Do not use stronger than the manufacturer's recommendation. Some gardeners consider sterile water best; others swear by a dash of a soft drink such as 7Up or Sprite.
6. For ease in arranging, you can use a wire netting balled up, pebbles, a metal holder, or a 'florists' porous foam. If using the foam:
    a. Saturate it thoroughly in advance in clean water, containing a floral preservative if desired. Most foams should not be reused.
    b. Use a vase large enough to permit submerging the block of foam.
    c. Be sure that the stem ends are below the surface of the water.
    d. Add water daily to replace that which is used by the flowers.
    e. Do not move the rose stem after inserting. To do so may leave an air pocket at the base of the stem.
    f. Keep the bouquet in a cool place out of direct sunlight and out of drafts.

These methods can also be used with roses from a florist.

HINT: Use a pipecleaner or soft wool to tie roses and hold until they are displayed (see illustration, p. 19).

Do It Yourself With Roses

Imitation Roses Materials for making imitation roses are as varied as the imagination. Below are instructions for a crepe paper rose but roses may also be made from tissue paper, silk, foil, woodfibre, wood, copper, silver or gold, clay, plaster, enamel, china, bread, icing, gumdrops, radishes, batik, organdy, wool, etc.

The Egyptians created the first artificial roses by cutting petals from thin wood chips which were then dyed red and scented with rose oil. Pliny tells us that later on they made roses from cloth and paper for exportation to Greece and Rome.

The English have always loved roses, none more so than Queen Alexandra. She suggested that artificial wild roses be sold on Alexandra Day in aid of hospitals. On her death, members of the Royal National Rose Society sent a magnificent wreath of roses.

Crepe Paper Roses
Piece of cardboard
Carbon paper
Cotton ball
Red and leaf green crepe paper
No. 23 wire
No. 16 stem wire or No. 18 garden stake
Green floral tape
White glue and brush
Scissors

Make patterns from the segments shown on the following page by tracing the design onto cardboard. Cut out the cardboard pattern and trace onto crepe paper. Be sure the paper's 'grain' runs along the length of the petals and leaves. Cut out petals.

To make the center for the rose, cover the cotton ball with a piece of red crepe paper. Close the opening by twisting with No. 23 wire and attach it to a No. 16 stem wire with green floral tape.

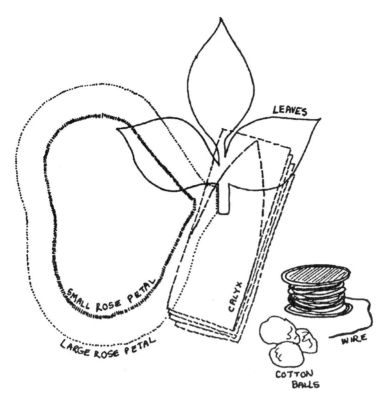

For one large rose, cut six small petals and seven large petals from red crepe paper. For a small rose, cut two small and two large petals.

Place your thumbs in the middle of each petal and cup it by stretching the crepe paper outward then bend the tips of each petal backward by rolling the paper much as you would curl a ribbon. The curved petals will stand away form the center like those of a fresh rose.

Use a brush to apply white glue one inch from the base area of each small petal. Hold the bud on the wire upside down. Glue on small petals first; then the larger petals. Be sure to space the petals evenly about the center. Avoid getting glue on the outside of the flower.

When all petals have been attached, accordion-fold a 3-by-20 inch piece of green crepe paper for the calyx (cup-like leaves at the base of each flower). To make calyx, cut along the curved dotted lines shown in pattern, leaving about 3/4 inch of the folded paper still joined at the base. Unfold the paper, and spread white glue 1/2 inch from the joined base of the paper. Wrap calyx around the bottom of the large outer rose petals.

Cut two pairs of leaves from green crepe paper. Glue each pair with a wire sandwiched vertically between. Allow 2 inches of wire to protrude.

In a spiral motion, wrap the entire stem with green floral tape. Start taping at the base of the calyx and work downward. Attach the leaves to the stem at intervals by wrapping each wire joint in with tape.

Freshen the completed rose petals and leaves by shaping them with the edge of a scissor or your fingertips.

Dried Roses

Preserve the fragile beauty of the roses you grew during the summer. Dried flowers are stiff and somewhat shrunken, but still colorful and beautiful. Use them for bouquets and table arrangements.

Drying flowers requires care, but is relatively easy to do.

Sand, Silica Gel or Kitty Litter Drying

Sand drying requires two weeks or so for total absorption of moisture from the roses. Silica gel takes only three or four days. Kitty litter takes about three weeks.

You can use the drying agents again but make sure to remove all moisture first by setting the drying agent in the sun or in the oven.

Sand sold for sand boxes or concrete can be used without special preparation. Seaside or lake sand must be washed to remove salt, then dried and sifted to remove foreign material.

Prepare flowers for drying as soon as possible after picking.

Empty shoe boxes are ideal containers for drying. A shoe box will accommodate one layer of largish flowers or two layers of smaller ones.

Large petalled or dense flowers, such as roses and dahlias, are dried face up. Pour enough sand or silica gel (one or two inches) into the drying container to support the flowers.

Cut off stems one inch below the blossoms. Insert a piece of wire into each for easier handling. Gently sift sand or gel over the flowers and into spaces between them. If the petals bend, hold them in place with fingers or a wooden dowel. Save the cut off portions of stem, insert wire into them, then place in the drying agent. You can re-attach them when the flowers are dry.

When thoroughly dry, remove the roses from the drying agent. You can start by pouring off the top layer, then carefully extracting the roses by hand. The dried roses are now ready to be re-wired to their stems, then formed into a long-lasting arrangement.

Run sand lightly over roses dried in gel to remove granules clinging to them. This is not necessary for flowers dried in sand. Push wires into the stems and wind with green florists tape. Re-attach any petals with white glue applied with a small brush. Store in an airtight container with the roses' stems stuck into florist foam to prevent crushing.

Dried Rose Arrangement

Like fresh roses, dried ones should be arranged with careful attention to color and form. You will need sand to weight your container, some floral foam and florist tape. Add wire extensions to stems whenever necessary to improve the flower's position. Anchor foam in sand. Insert the stems of the roses into the foam.

How to Press Flowers and Leaves

Use absorbent paper like newspaper or paper towels (don't use paper with an embossed pattern on the back as this will give a waffled texture to the roses).

Fold the paper. Put the roses and leaves between the fold. They will dry exactly as you place them; if you want a curved stem or flower, put them on the paper in that position. Flowers, leaves and stems can be pressed separately and reassembled if you choose.

Now put the folded paper under a heavy weight—a large book, or board and stone.

The length of time it takes for the materials to dry depends on atmospheric conditions and thickness of petals.

Placemats and Coasters

Start with a plain placemat, cardboard or felt and add rose petal design using lampshade method. Attach plastic film front and back. You can try a heavy rose-patterned fabric instead of real petals.

Rose Lamp Shade

By attaching rose petals to an old lamp shade you can have a rosy glow almost as quickly as you switch on the light.

Old lamp shade

Pressed rose petals and leaves

Clear all-purpose glue

Clear laminating film (available at hobby or art supply shops)

Carefully disassemble the old shade removing the fabric (parchment, silk, etc.) and laying it out flat. Spread pressed flowers in a pleasing design on the flattened shade and glue them there. Then cover shade with laminating film. Gently curl the shade back to the size and shape it was before.

To fasten the shade back together, either glue one edge of it on top of itself, or lace the edges together with heavy thread, cord, leather or plastic strips.

When you curl the shade back to its original size it should fit snugly around the wire frame again. Glue the wire to the shade or use the same lacing you used for the side.

Stand back and enjoy your rosy handwork.

IMPORTANT: It is vital to dry flowers completely. Otherwise the heat from the electric light will dry them out too rapidly and cause unattractive color changes.

Wallpaper

Don't be afraid to paper a room with one of the latest romantic rose-patterned wallpapers. Or try a flamboyant pattern framed on one painted wall.

The old joke from the 1930's Depression days; "take down the wallpaper, we're moving"— has become a reality; you can now buy wallpaper that can be easily removed, then applied to another surface.

Another idea is to create your own wallpaper by blowing up your favorite rose photograph.

Screens are currently a popular decorator item. You could use your blow-up on a screen. Or create a screen from a montage of roses cut from greeting cards, seed catalogues or wallpaper.

3

China & Silverware

This Queen of Flowers, as Sappho named the rose, has been perpetuated in faience by the designers of pottery plates, bowls and tiles. In Shiraz, the interior of a magnificent tiled mosque was completely covered with the design of roses, with every shade of pink in the blooms and green malachite and emeralds forming the leaves.

From the 18th century onwards enamel patch boxes were decorated with roses entwined with doves and a sentimental motto, or a single full-blown rose. They were made in England and France.

It was from the Egyptians that the Greeks and Romans acquired the habit of anointing their heads and bodies, strewing their rooms with flowers, and decorating their wine goblets with wreaths. They also acquired the habit of scenting their earthenware drinking cups. The perfume was mixed with the clay before it was baked.

Porcelain The light Vincennes style of china was used by Sevres Pottery, where dainty enamelled sprigs and sprays of flowers were painted onto plain white porcelain. Porcelain-de-lune, made for presentation purposes, was later developed; strong, ground colors were used leaving reserves of white porcelain visible in a sort of cartouche in which flowers or scenes after Boucher and Watteau were painted. The first ground color used was gros bleu. Then came rose Pompadour, sometimes called rose du Barry, invented by the chemist Xhrouet in 1757.

British Porcelain & Bone China

Lowestoft

As with all early porcelain-makers, the first efforts of Lowestoft painters were entirely dominated by oriental motifs. Eventually all painters expanded into more European designs and among the most frequent of Lowestoft decorative motifs was the rose.

The popularity of the rose at Lowestoft is explained by the fact that the rose is part of the coat of arms of the old borough. A decorator named Thomas Rose is considered to have been responsible for many of the later roses in red, chocolate, pink and purple. The finest painting of bouquets and sprays was done between 1773 and 1780.

Coalport

Under John Rose (J. Rose and Co.) a series of wide-mouthed jugs in various sizes, often painted with large pink roses, were a Coalport specialty of 1828 -1840.

Coalport was the first English pottery to obtain the famous 'rose Pompadour' color. A rare Coalport mark is a rose, the mark of John or W. Rose.

In the 18th century European importers were ordering porcelain directly from China with European designs, including roses. Perfection in the use of opaque enamels of the 'famille rose' palette after their discovery in 1720, provided the Chinese decorators with a full range of colors with which to satisfy their export trade.

Kirkcaldy

The Rosette pattern from Kirkcaldy pottery of Scotland began in the 18th century. Sometimes known as Pink Posy, it is the most common Kirkcaldy pattern and is found in tableware, toiletries and bowls. The pottery was finally closed in 1930 after a large percentage of the ware was shipped to America, particularly Canada.

Staffordshire

The 19th century Kings Rose Pattern shows a large orange or red cabbage rose. The Queens Rose is a pink rose.

Rose Tapestry

Rose tapestry was the most popular and prevalent floral motif used on a 'matte finish' china made in the 19th century. Rose tapestry china, which has a rough effect that feels like woven cloth, was made by wrapping the article in coarse cloth and then firing. The cloth was consumed in the firing, and the tapestry effect remained.

Rose tapestry ranges from pale pink to deeper red colors, occasionally with pale yellow or white roses. The rarest rose tapestry is 'sterling silver'. The roses range in color from a deep gray to a pale silver gray shaded into white.

Modern Rose China Patterns

For decades, Royal Albert 'Old Country Rose' has been the world-wide largest-selling rose-patterned china. With large red, yellow and pink roses and a lavish gold border, it is the most realistic of designs. Old Country Rose is also used on lamps, giftware and desk sets. Salt and pepper shakers were once made with a full blown rose at the top for the salt and pepper to be shaken out of.

In 1988 'American Beauty', a large pink rose design, was re-issued. 'Beauty' now out-sells the perennial favorite according to Eaton's china department in Vancouver.

A new blue rose called 'Moonlight Blue' is the same pattern as Old Country Rose and some collectors are mixing the two designs for table settings.

Many of the new rose designs are geometric and stylized roses combined with bands and stripes for an art deco look. A few patterns by various potteries are:

> *Paragon*: 'First Love' (small white sprays) and 'Victoria Rose' (small pink nosegays)
>
> *Royal Doulton*: 'Twilight Rose' (art deco pale pink and geometric) and 'Winter Rose' (grey, long-stemmed rose with a black border)
>
> *Minton:* 'Chartwell' and 'Sunningdale' (small rose prints)
>
> *Wedgewood*: 'Conway' (one of the few rose designs from this pottery)
>
> *Royal Albert*: 'Lavender Rose' (sprays of small pink roses)

English bone china has a tradition of rose patterns, and tea sets are still available in rose designs. Evoking images of English high tea in lovely gardens with women in long white dresses and men in flannels and boaters, these patterns remain ever popular.

Collector Plates

For many years a popular collectors item has been the collector plate and roses are a lasting favorite design. The Boehm Studios of Edward Marshall alone has over 30 rose designs, many of them award winning.

Other famous editions include:

King's porcelain of Italy, high relief, 3-dimensional plates.

King's 'Red Roses', in the 'Flowers of America' series.

Pickard of the United States rose editions.

Plates are listed from about $50 up to $100. Consult your library for the latest Official Collector Plate price guide.

China Figurines

The famous Royal Doulton figurines include the Old Country Rose design as well as many other dainty rose patterns in red, pink, peach, blue and yellow.

Silver

Silver pieces popular around the turn of the century included tea sets in a simple rose design, berry bowls with handles of wild roses and the Queen of Flowers dressing table set with a nude figure in the art nouveau style surrounded by entwined roses.

Old silver flatware includes dozens of rose patterns, among them:

'Bride': 1909, Holmes & Edwards, an ornate pattern with groups of roses.

'Bride's Bouquet': 1908, Gorham-Alvin, a delicate design with ribbons from the bouquet flowing down the handle.

'Rosalie': 1905, Royal Plate, single full roses with leaves.

'Jac Rose': 1892, International, Holmes & Edwards, one large and one small rose intertwined with feathery leaves.

'American Beauty Rose': 1909, various manufacturers, compact groups of roses and leaves.

'*Modern Rose*': 1949, Rogers & Bros., a linear design with a tangle of roses down the centre.

'*Moss Rose*': 1949, National Silver Co., roses reminiscent of early wild roses with a trail of greenery.

'*Morning Rose*': 1960, Oneida-Community, a sweeping design with a long-stemmed rose and bud.

'*Dresden Rose*': 1953, Reed & Barton, dainty, miniature rose border.

There are many more choices, both old and new. Silver and stainless steel flatware rose patterns continue to be manufactured.

Do It Yourself with Roses
Your Dinner Table

It is not necessary to have a complete rose patterned dinner set. For a both unusual and fanciful table, try collecting cups, saucers, plates and silverware in a myriad of mix and match rose patterns.

China Painting

When painting china, the technique is to paint and fire several times to obtain the necessary effect. Do not apply the paint so thick as to destroy the translucency of the china

Materials

- Onglaze colors: These are pigments made from metallic and mineral oxides and used to decorate porcelain and china. There are one or two colors which are used constantly by china painters and which have become synonymous with a certain color, for example American Beauty (deep damson pink) and Ashes of Roses (grey-pink). With experience you will develop the palette which rose painting dictates.

  Pre-mixed water-based colors are best for the beginner, progressing to powdered colors into which a 'medium' or oil is mixed.

Other basics include:

- Chinagraph pencil: A soft pencil suitable for drawing on china and

glass; it will burn off during the firing process. Choose a fine one.
- Graphite paper: A special light texture carbon paper for transferring designs to china.
- Palette: Mixed colors must be covered to avoid contamination by dust and lint: Ready made palettes are available but a cookie tin with a lid is a good substitute.
- 6 inch pure silk and cotton wool: Make into small balls and cover with two layers of silk for a pad (to use instead of a brush) to paint a smooth background.
- Wipe-out tool: A stick with two little rubber pointed ends to wipe out highlights etc.
- Turpentine: This must be the pure spirits of turps not the household variety. Turps is used to clean your brushes and palette.
- Brushes: Your most important tool. Always buy the best you can afford and look after them! Clean with pure turps after every use. Dry and condition with a fine smear of olive-oil, re-shape and store in a dustproof container.

Roses have a reputation for being difficult to paint, but the problems can be overcome with practice. There are many ways of painting roses but a few basic rules can be given (also see Painting a Rose in the VISUAL ARTS section).

The following are some tips for the amateur potter or ceramist who wishes to experiment with a rose design on ready-glazed white china.
1. Preferably paint from life.
2. Use a tile to practice on.
3. Practice with one color.
4. Begin at the centre of the rose.
5. Lightly shape the rounding of the outer petals.
6. Rounded shapes of the brushwork must follow the curves of the petals.
7. For light highlights use wipe-out tool or dip brush in turpentine to remove pigment.
8. For shading, keep brush strokes as simple and airy as possible.

Suggested colors: rose pink, ruby pink, yellow-green, shading green, blue-green, baby blue, Albert yellow, brown.

NOTE: The real difficulty in painting roses lies in making them as light as possible, and that is achieved only by using the white color of the china as an element of the painting.

WORLD ORGANIZATION OF CHINA PAINTERS, 3111,19th Street, Oklahoma City, OK. 73107, Contact: Pauline Salyer, Magazine: 'The China Painter'

4

Food

The rose is such an ornamental flower that few people look upon it as an important herb. Yet few plants have been used as much in the kitchen and by druggists as the rose. It has been eaten in one way or another since recipes were first written. Growing roses in the kitchen garden was common until the 17th century.

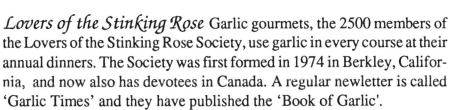

At a dinner presided over by Lord Leyster, Chancellor of Oxford University in 1570, there is an account "for rose water for boyled meates and to wash afore dinner and after dinner, 2s. 9d.".

Lovers of the Stinking Rose Garlic gourmets, the 2500 members of the Lovers of the Stinking Rose Society, use garlic in every course at their annual dinners. The Society was first formed in 1974 in Berkley, California, and now also has devotees in Canada. A regular newletter is called 'Garlic Times' and they have published the 'Book of Garlic'.
P.S. Roses love garlic as a companion plant. Planted near roses, garlic aids in fighting black spot.

Main Dishes

Chicken a la Rose
Serves 4

2 chicken breasts, split
Generous pinch each of ginger, salt, pepper
4 tbsp. butter plus 2 tbsp.
1/2 tsp. lemon juice
1/3 cup honey
1 tbsp. rosewater
2 tbsp. chopped rose petals

Remove skin, wash and dry chicken, then rub with ginger, salt and pepper. Melt 4 tbsp. butter in a saute pan and when it starts to foam add the chicken and brown on both sides. Then place chicken in casserole.

To the juices in the saute pan add 2 tbsp. butter, lemon juice, honey and rosewater. Blend well over heat. Pour over the chicken, cover casserole and bake at 325°F until fork tender (about 30–40 minutes). Baste occasionally.

Place chicken on a serving platter, sprinkle with rose petals and spoon remaining juices over all.

Rosey Glazed Carrots
Serves 4

2 cups cooked baby carrots (or sliced carrots)
2 tbsp. honey
2 tbsp. butter
1 tbsp. rose jelly (or ginger jelly)
1 tbsp. rosewater

Cook carrots until tender. Drain. Set aside. In separate pan melt butter and add other ingredients. Simmer three minutes. Add carrots. Simmer one more minute.

NOTE: Be imaginative and try with other vegetables such as zucchini.

Rose Rice
Serves 4

3 tbsp. butter
1/4 cup minced onion
1 cup rice
2 to 3 tbsp. fresh rose petals (1 to 2 tbsp. crushed dried)
2 cups chicken stock
Salt and pepper to taste

Melt butter in heavy skillet; saute onion until translucent, add rice and saute until each grain is well coated. Sprinkle the rose petals on the broth to soften and then add to the rice mixture along with salt and pepper. Cover and simmer about 20 minutes.

Spreads & Dips

Use finely ground dried petals in cottage or cream cheese, sour cream, or other spreads. Use alone or with parsley and/or dill.

Rose Butter

In a glass dish place a layer of fragrant rose petals, then one half of 1/4 pound stick of sweet butter, sliced lengthwise. Add another layer of petals, the rest of the butter, and cover with remaining petals. Cover tightly and allow to stand at normal room temperature for an hour. Refrigerate.

The next day remove petals and cream butter before using. (If you prefer, put butter with petals through the blender).

If you do not have rose petals, cream together one stick of butter and one tsp. of strong rosewater.

Rose Butter can be used for sandwiches or spread on bread with thinly sliced chicken, meat or crab meat.

Rose Sandwich

Butter the bread, fill with fresh rose petals and refrigerate. Add sprouts or honey if desired.

Rose Tea Sandwich

(makes 24–32 tea sandwiches)
16 slices bread (crusts removed)
1/4 lb. butter
4 tbsp. minced rose petals
1 tbsp. rose vinegar
1 tbsp. rose syrup (or honey)
1/2 cup minced chicken
2 tbsp. ground, toasted almonds
Salt and pepper to taste

Slice the bread very thin. Combine other ingredients for filling. Complete sandwiches, cut into quarters (or thirds) and top each tiny sandwich with a bit of minced parsley and additional minced rose petals.

Salads, Soups, Dressings & Garnishes

Petals are nice to nibble on. They enhance fruit and vegetable salads, soups and purees. Ground or powdered, they can be used in all cooked foods: soup, baked or broiled meats, casseroles, baked goods, jellies and preserves, sauces, fruit molds and even omelettes.

Rosy Salad

Rose petals
Fresh fruit
Fresh lime juice

Toss petals and fruit. Sprinkle with freshly squeezed lime juice and (if desired), Confectio Rosae Gallicae (See ROSE DESSERTS AND CANDIED PETALS section for Confectio recipe).

Tangy Salad Dressing

1/4 cup rose vinegar
1/4 cup olive oil
Shake together.

Rose Vinegar

(Also see ROSEWATER and ROSE VINEGAR recipes in COSMETIC
  section)

Steep 1 oz. each of rose petals and chamomile in white wine vinegar for at least two weeks. Strain and add 1 cup of rosewater. Add other spices if desired. Use generously on salads.

Pickled Rosebuds

Rosebuds to fill a pint jar
1/2 cup sugar
2 cups white vinegar
Mace or mint sprigs (optional)

Wash rosebuds and fill jar. Cover with boiling sugar/vinegar mixture. Add sprigs of mace or mint. Seal.

Pickled rosebuds are ready in two weeks to garnish a relish tray or serve with crab, lobster or chicken salad. After opening, keep refrigerated. The chopped buds go well in green salads, coleslaw and as a sandwich ingredient.

Useful Rose Hip Puree

Remove the blossom and stem ends of each hip. Add about 1 pint water for each pound of hips and cook until tender (about 20 minutes) in a covered enamel or glass saucepan. Press the mixture through a sieve. Store in glass container in refrigerator.

This puree can be used to flavor soups, mixed with puddings or served with stewed meats or vegetables.

Rose Hip Soup

The Swedes make a fruit soup, called Nypon-Soppa, which is served either hot or cold at the beginning of a meal. It is easy to make.

3 cups fresh or 2 cups dry rose hips
3 pints water
3/4 cup sugar
Salt
1 1/2 tbsp. potato flour
1/4 cup shredded almonds

With scissors remove tops and bottoms of hips. Chop or grind them. Place in boiling water. Cover and cook until tender; then strain, forcing the hips through a sieve.

Take 4 1/2 cups liquid from this process (add cold water if needed to make full amount). Return to kettle, add sugar and a dash of salt and stir in potato flour which has been mixed with a little water to make a smooth paste. Bring to a boil, stirring constantly.

Pour into a soup tureen and add almonds. Chill. This soup is served cold in Sweden but may be served hot.

Garnish with whipped cream and serve with rusks which are crumbled into soup.

NOTE: Dry rose hips or packaged ready-to-eat Nypon-soppa can be purchased in Scandinavian food stores.

Rose Desserts and Candied Petals

The Greeks grew roses and the ancient Egyptians offered flowers to their gods, but it was the Romans who adored them in a way that has never been rivaled.

Rose petals garlanded their heads and floated in their wine. There were rose honeys, rose wines and rose puddings. Fresh roses were used as an aphrodisiac.

The following excerpt is from the customs and practices of the Regiment XX Lancashire Fusiliers:

> *The dinner table is decorated with roses. Officers wear*
> *one red and one yellow rose...After the loyal toast has*
> *been drunk and glasses refilled, the President, when*
> *required by the Commanding Officer rings his handbell,*
> *and the Commanding Officer rises and proposes the Minden*
> *Toast in the words*
> *"We will now rise and drink in solemn*
> *silence to those who fell at Minden."*
> *Later, when the Bandmaster has been entertained and the*
> *waiters have withdrawn, the President orders the Mess*
> *Sergeant to place, with the President's compliments, a*
> *rose in front of each officer who has not previously eaten*
> *one with a Minden Regiment. As soon as the roses are put*
> *before them, these officers rise and eat the roses. The*
> *roses are served in champagne . . . Officers eating roses*
> *stand on their chairs, but do not put a foot on the table;*

*they remain standing on their chairs till they have eaten
the rose and drunk the champagne. When there are only a
few officers to eat roses, they are handed them in
succession as each one finishes; but when there are
several officers the roses are given them in quick
succession before the previous one has finished. Custom
does not require an officer to eat a rose at a Minden
Dinner more than once during his service."*

Today we use fragrant rose petals in salads, as garnishes, candied to decorate pastries, and to make rosewater which is used in East Indian and Arabic cuisines.

Rose hips, the fruit of the rose, are just as popular in today's cuisine. Tart and cranberrylike, they're famous for their high vitamin C content and are used to make syrups, jellies, jams, conserves, teas, wines, pies, tarts, quick breads and muffins.

Candied Roses
1 egg white
1 tbsp. cold water
Finely granulated sugar

Lightly beat egg white with water. Dip roses into the mixture. Set the dipped roses on a tray and sprinkle with finely granulated sugar to cover all surfaces. Allow to dry and store in air tight cans in a cool place. Use as an edible garnish.

NOTE: Other flowers and leaves can be preserved in the same manner.

Confectio Rosae Gallicae
(Rose sugar)
10 oz. fresh rose petals
30 oz. refined sugar

Beat together in stone mortar or blender.

NOTE: Like vinegar, sugar is a fine preserving agent. Candied herbs, especially flowers have been used as garnishes for centuries.

Rosewater Meringues

These meringues can be made well in advance and stored in an airtight container.

Whites of six large eggs
2 1/4 cups (1 lb.) superfine sugar
1 1/2 tsp. rosewater
1 1/2 tsp. vinegar

Pre-heat oven to 200° F. Brush baking sheets with oil and dredge with flour. Shake off excess.

Beat egg whites in large mixing bowl until they hold stiff peaks. Still beating, gradually add 2 tbsp. sugar. Beat well. Add remaining sugar, 2 tbsp. at a time, and continue beating until mixture is shiny and holds stiff peaks. Mix rosewater and vinegar; fold into egg mixture with a metal spoon. Spoon small amounts of mixture onto the baking sheets.

Before placing meringues in oven, turn down heat to lowest setting, preferably 150° F. Cook for two hours. Remove baking sheets and turn off oven. Carefully loosen meringues and return to oven for another 30 minutes. Cool on wire rack. Store in airtight containers. Serve by themselves or with fruit, ice cream, whipped cream or a sauce.

Genoese Rose Cream
(Sinfully delicious party fare.)

2 cups hot milk
Small amount cold milk
1 heaping tbsp. flour
2 tbsp. sugar
Piece of butter half the size of an egg
3 beaten egg yolks
Rose flavoring
1/2 lb. almonds
Sponge cake
Sweet wine

Blanch almonds, chop fine and set aside.

Blend sugar, flour and butter in saucepan. Gradually add a small amount of cold milk. Then slowly blend in hot milk and simmer 10 minutes. Stir in beaten egg yolk, remove from heat and cool slightly. Add rose flavoring to taste. Stir in one half of the chopped almonds.

Dip slices of sponge cake into the wine and lay in a decorative dessert bowl. Pour the batter over the cake and spread the remaining almonds over the top. Garnish with candied roses. Serve with rose flavored whipped cream.

Cake with Roses

Try this for a bridal shower or a birthday party.

In centre of table put a rose-flavored sponge cake, with rose icing, that has been baked in an angel-cake tin (with hole in centre). Put a small glass in the centre hole and fill with a bouquet of roses.

Around the bottom of the cake, make a circle of single rose corsages, one for each guest (conceal a corsage pin in each). To each rose corsage, tie a pink ribbon long enough to reach each guest's place at the table. When it is time to cut the cake, each guest pulls a rose corsage to her and wears it.

Dessert Wafers

From 'The Receipt Book of John Nott', Cook to the Duke of Bolton, 1723.

To Make Wafers: Put the yolks of four eggs, and three Spoonfuls of Rose-water, to a quart of flour; mingle them well, make them into a Batter with cream and double-refined sugar, pour it on very thin, and bake it on Irons. (These sound wonderful for filling with rosewater-flavored whipped cream and strawberries!)

Rose Ice Cream

2 cups vanilla ice cream
1/3 cup red rose petals
1/3 cup cranberry juice
1 tbsp. lemon juice

Let ice cream stand at room temperature until soft enough to stir. Blend petals, lemon and cranberry juice in blender. Stir mixture into ice cream. Pour into a freezer tray. Stir occasionally until firm.

Turkish Delight

This Eastern delicacy is known around the world as one of the oldest recipes using rosewater.

2 tbsp. gelatine powder
1 1/4 cups water
1 tsp. strong rosewater
2 2/3 cups sugar
A few drops vanilla or peppermint essence
A few drops cochineal
1/4 cup chopped nuts (optional)
1/4 cup icing sugar
1/4 cup cornstarch

Lightly grease a 7 or 8 inch square cake pan.

Place gelatine, water, rosewater and sugar in saucepan. Heat gently, stirring constantly, until the gelatine and sugar are completely dissolved. Increase the heat and bring to boil, without stirring. Immediately reduce heat and leave to simmer for 20–25 minutes. Remove from the heat. Stir in flavoring and coloring and leave to cool for 5 minutes.

Quickly stir in the nuts and pour into the prepared cake pan. Leave 24 hours to set firm before cutting into squares. Toss the squares in mixed sieved icing sugar and cornstarch. Pack into an airtight container, sprinkling extra sugar and flour between layers.

Rose Flavored Nuts

Nuts can be lightly flavored with flowers. Rose petals, carnations or violets work well. Almost fill a tall jar with several kinds of nuts. Make sure they aren't salty or stale. Stir in the petals and buds of roses and seal the jar with wax paper and a rubber band. Let stand in a cool place and stir every few days. No nibbling until a week has passed!

Rose-Drops

2 cups berry sugar
1 oz. dried red roses
Lemon juice

Grind the roses to a fine powder in blender. Mix together with the sugar and enough lemon juice to make a stiff paste. Set over low heat, stirring well, and when scalding hot remove from heat and drop in small portions on wax paper. Let set.

Jams & Syrups

It is to the Arabs we owe many of our delicious syrups, sherbets, juleps, fragrant flavoring waters and conserves of scented flowers.

When using rose petals in such recipes, it is recommended that you remove the white portion at the base of the petal.

Try storing the syrups in soft drink bottles with screw-on caps. Pour the hot syrup all the way to the top of the bottles and cap each one as you fill it. Use an exotic rose label.

Rose Petal Syrup

4 cups rose petals
2 cups water
2 cups sugar
1/4 tsp. powdered cloves
Beet juice (optional)

Simmer rose petals, water, sugar and cloves for one hour. Add few drops beet juice for color. Strain through fine sieve (or nylon stocking). Bottle and cap.

Easy Rose Syrup

Rosewater
Honey
Beet juice (optional)
Rose extract (optional)

Thicken rosewater with honey in blender. For extra color add some beet juice. For extra flavor add some rose extract. Use on pancakes, waffles, toasts, ice cream and other desserts.

Honey of Roses

1 cup red rose petals
1 cup water
1 cup honey
1 tbsp. beet juice (optional)
1/4 tsp. rose extract (optional)

Measure water and rose petals in blender. Blend well. Bring mixture to boil then reduce heat and simmer five minutes. Strain through a fine sieve or double thickness nylon.

Reheat the strained mixture with honey, stirring constantly until dissolved and hot, but do not boil. Remove from heat and stir in beet juice and rose extract. Use as a spread, a topping on pancakes and in hot or cold drinks.

Strawberry Rose Syrup

1 cup Honey of Roses syrup (as above)
1 cup fresh strawberries

Puree strawberries in blender. With blender on low speed, gradually add Honey of Roses syrup. This is a tempting topping for ice cream or yogurt sundaes.

Rose Petal Jam

2 cups dark red rose petals, crushed
1 tbsp. sugar
2 tbsp. lemon juice
4 cups sugar
3/4 cup water
 1 tbsp. lemon juice

Sprinkle rose petals with 1 tbsp. sugar and 2 tbsp. lemon juice. Crush down to reduce bulk.

Combine 4 cups sugar and water in pot. Bring to boil. Add petals, simmer approximately 10 minutes, stirring frequently. Add 1 tbsp. lemon juice. Leave 12 hours. Bring to boil again, simmer until thick and clear. Pack into jars. Seal. Store in a cool dark place.

Rose petal jam served inside thin folded pancakes is a classic dessert of the Middle East.

No Cook Rose Jam

1 cup red or pink petals (firmly packed)
3/4 bottle liquid pectin
1 tbsp. lemon juice
2 tbsp. honey

Blend for a few seconds on low speed and store in refrigerator.

Ginger Rose Hip Jam

1 1/2 cups rose hip puree
2 cups sugar
1/2 cup pineapple, finely diced
2 tbsp. lemon juice
1 tbsp. minced crystallized ginger

Combine all the ingredients in a saucepan and cook over medium heat, stirring constantly, until the jam thickens. Pour into hot sterilized jars and seal. Makes 3 half-pint jars.

Rose Hip Jelly

2 lbs. rosehips
5 cups water
2 cups sugar (approx.)
3 tbsp. lemon juice, or to taste

Wash the rosehips and chop roughly. Put them in a pan with the water and boil for about one hour or until soft. Put in a jelly bag and leave to drip overnight.

Next day, measure juice and add 2 cups of sugar to every 2 1/2 cups of juice. Heat slowly in a pan until the sugar has dissolved, then boil steadily until setting point is reached. Skim off surface scum, add lemon juice to taste and pour into small jars. Seal when cool. Makes about 1 1/2 pounds.

For a special dessert, fill crepes with a spoonful of rose jelly and garnish with candied or fresh rose petals.

Uses of Rosewater

(See recipe in COSMETIC section)
1. Flavor whipped creams and icings.
2. Use instead of liquid in making cakes, breads, pies, puddings, sauces or gelatins.
3. Use in syrups.

In our great grandmothers' time, fragrant damask rose petals were put into cherry pies before putting on the crusts. In earlier days rosewater was used to flavor cakes.

5

Drinks

Today, we are far more likely to associate aromas such as rose and lavender with soaps and perfumes. Commercial alcoholic beverages made from flowers have become almost obsolete.

Yet, most old cookbooks from England, Italy and France have recipes for alcoholic drinks made with flowers. Awaiting you are new taste thrills as you experiment with the following old-fashioned style of beverage made from fresh flowers picked from your own garden. Experiment, always thinking of other ingredients that might be added.

Pick the flowers while in full bloom and separate them from their leaves, stamens and stems. Gently rinse and pat dry.

One method of making a floral liqueur is to steep the petals in vodka, strain, and then add a sweetener and spices. You can also combine other herb liqueurs with flower petals to alter or perk up the taste.

Liqueurs and Wines

Basic Rose Liqueur Recipe
(2 to 2 1/2 cup yield)

1 1/2 cups fresh fragrant rose petals or 1/3 cup dried petals
1 1/2 cups vodka
1/2 cup sugar syrup (recipe below)
Wash fresh rose petals and dab dry on paper towels. Steep petals in vodka 2 to 3 weeks. Strain and squeeze out juices. Add sugar syrup. Let mature approximately one week.

Optional additions: cardamom, lemon peel, orange peel, caraway, cherries, apple, peaches, pears, plums, raspberries.

Generally vodkas are 80/proof. If 100/proof, increase sugar syrup by one eighth.

Glycerine is used by commercial liqueur makers as a 'smoother' to help it roll off your tongue. If you choose, add approx. 1 tsp. per quart of finished liqueur. Shake well.

Syrup
2 parts sugar
1 part water

Bring to boil, stirring until sugar dissolves—about 5 minutes. Always cool before adding to alcohol or it will evaporate.

The liqueurs can be stored in dark beer bottles (thoroughly cleaned and sterilized) to mature. More decorative bottles can be used for gift giving. Buy corks to fit, and make your own rose labels.

The visual taste sensation will be greater if you add a few drops of any pure food coloring sold for cooking and baking.

NOTE: Petals strained from the liqueur can be used for brewing tea.

Liqueur using Essential Oil
25 oz. vodka
1/2 rounded tsp. glycerin
40 drops pure rose essential oil
Stir well and add 1/2 to 1 cup of sugar syrup

Cover the container with a tight lid and stir occasionally over several days. The quantities of syrup and essential oil may be varied according to taste.

Wine of Rose
1 pint red wine
1 pint red rosebuds and petals

Put rosebuds and petals in glass jar. Add wine a little at a time, shaking the mixture well. Seal and let stand 4 or 5 days. Shake it twice a day. Stir and strain, pressing out all essence. Use as a cocktail or marinade.

Rose Petal Wine

2 quarts rose petals
2 lbs. sugar
1/2 pint white grape concentrate
Wine yeast—Champagne, Hock or Bordeaux
1 gallon water
Campden tablets (50 ppm. sulfite)
Additives (for one gallon)
      12 mg.Benerva (Vitamin B1 tablets)
      1 heaped tsp. citric acid
      1/4 oz. tartaric acid
      1/2 tsp. grape tannin or tannic acid
      1 tsp. ammonium phosphate or 1 nutrient tablet
Advisable: 1 tsp. pectinol, or pectolase

Put roses in plastic bucket with sugar, grape concentrate and additives. Pour on 6 pints of cold water. Stir thoroughly to dissolve sugar, etc. Add one Campden tablet and cover. Leave for 24 hours. After 24 hours add yeast, and ferment on the flowers for four days at a temperature of approximately 70°F (21°C). Strain the liquid into a gallon jar and fit a bored cork with an airlock plugged with cotton wool. Raise temperature, if possible, to 75°F (24°C).

Ferment to dryness, i.e. the gravity should fall below the zero mark. Rack into a fresh jar, and top up with water (if necessary), add one Campden tablet, fit a bored cork tightly plugged with cotton wool.

This wine becomes drinkable after a few weeks, but improves with maturing up to 2 years. The wine requires sweetening with up to 1/2 lb. sugar per gallon. NOTE: Dried rose petals can be used if fresh unavailable. The approximate equivalent of 5 pints of fresh petals is one ounce (by weight) of dried crushed petals.

If red petals are used the final color will be a light rose color. Add food coloring if desired. For a white wine use white or yellow petals.

Brandy Rose Wine

1/2 lb. red rose petals
1 pint hot water
1 lb. sugar
1/2 pint brandy

Mix fragrant red petals with hot water and squeeze through a fine sieve. Add more petals until the liquid is a rich red color and then stir in sugar and brandy. Bottle and serve as soon as you like.

Rose Ice Cubes

Gather fresh colored rose petals, wash well and chop most of them up finely. Save a whole petal for each cube. Mix chopped petals in water and then pour into ice cube trays and freeze. When cubes are partially set, slide a rose petal into each one. Leave to finish freezing. Mint leaves are also a good choice for a decorative ice cube.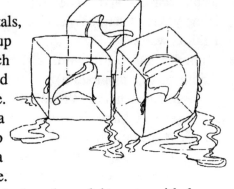

When flavored ice cubes are desired, replace plain water with: lemonade, limeade, apple juice, or diluted rosewater.

NOTE: To use as a decoration or to keep salads fresh on a buffet table, freeze the cubes in your deep freeze instead of the refrigerator. They will last longer.

To decorate a punch bowl, fill a large container (such as a margarine container) with water or juice. Insert whole rosebuds, petals and leaves. Freeze in deep freeze.

Rose Aperitif for Two

1 cup watermelon, seeded and cubed
2 tbsp. Rosewater Syrup (recipe below)
3 oz. vodka

Chill ingredients well. Combine with 3 to 4 crushed ice cubes in blender for 20 seconds. Serve in a brandy snifter with a straw, topped with a rose bud, rose petal or candied rose.

Rosewater Syrup

2 cups sugar
1 cup light corn syrup
1/2 cup water
4 tbsp. rosewater
red food coloring

Boil water, sugar and syrup. Stir constantly until it spins a thread when dropped from a spoon. Remove from heat. Cool. Stir in rosewater

and a drop or two of red food coloring for desired shade. Use in cooling drinks, in whipped cream, on pancakes, fresh fruits and desserts.
NOTE: For other Rose Syrup recipes see JAMS section.

Raspberry Rose Punch

1 cup rosewater
Rind of one lemon, grated
1/2 cup brown sugar (or honey)
1 pint crushed raspberries
2 tbsp. lemon juice
4 cups water (or gingerale or soda water)

Heat sugar, rosewater and lemon rind over low heat until sugar is dissolved. Simmer 5 minutes without stirring. Remove from heat and add crushed raspberries. Strain. Cool. When ready to serve, add the lemon juice and 4 cups of water. Pour over ice in a pitcher or tall glasses. Or reheat and serve as a hot punch.

Teas

Herb teas are gaining in popularity because they soothe without sedating and refresh without the nerve jangling effects of drinks with caffeine.

Teas composed of garden grown herbs are as varied as the imagination. A little experimental brewing and sipping are sure to result in a special blend or two.

Among the most exotic flowers for the teapot are roses, although it is the vitamin C rich rose hip that is most often brewed. The species Rosa rugosa and its many named selections produce some of the biggest and most prolific hips. Scabrosa, a four foot shrub (whose flowers are mallow pink with creamy stamens), produces large orange-red hips. Jens Munk, 5-6 feet tall (wine-colored flowers), has marble sized crimson hips.

Rose Hip Tea

Pick hips when they are plump and red but not softly over-ripe. Remove stalks and blossom ends. Cut in half. Let dry until brittle. Store in a sealed container.

To make tea: Pulverize a handful in blender or mill. Use one cup of boiling water to one teaspoon of rose hip pulp. Let steep 10 minutes. Strain. Sweeten with honey.

Rose hips (the fruit of roses) contain 6 to 8 times more vitamin C than oranges. A handful of hips contains as much as 60 oranges. Great cold prevention.

Rose Hip Tea Blend

1 cup dried rose hips
1 three-inch stick cinnamon
1/4 cup dried lemon balm leaves
1 tsp. dried, grated organic lemon rind

Other Rose Blends

The proportion for tea blends is usually equal parts, except for spices which are overpowering. Your taste buds are the best judge.

1. Spearmint, alfalfa, chamomile, rosebuds
2. Spearmint, rose hips, sage
3. Lemon verbena, chamomile, rose hips
4. Wild cherry bark, rose hips, hibiscus, spearmint, lemongrass, orange peel
5. Lemon verbena, rosebuds, chamomile, rosemary

To make Tea

Use one teaspoon of blend to one cup boiling water. Use a china, glass or enamel teapot. Steep flowers or leaves five to 10 minutes. Seeds, roots and barks should be simmered 10 minutes. Strain and serve with honey if desired.

Rose Petal Tea

A freshly made tea of dried rose petals is a pleasant cooling drink on warm summer days. Collect the petals to be dried before the flower unfolds. Use 2 heaping teaspoons per cup of boiling water.

6

Perfuming the House

Perfuming the house means to take pleasure in your sense of smell. Smell is often the strongest impression a visitor has of your home. Odor memory is better than visual; once remembered, smells are rarely forgotten.

Our sense of smell was the first of our senses to evolve; the smell-receptor nerves feed directly into the thinking area of our brain, meaning that our noses give us our most immediate and intimate contact with the outside world.

For the rose lover, then, what better way to evoke what you want to say about yourself and your lifestyle than to permeate the air with roses.

The Aromatic Household

That which we call a rose by any other name
would smell as sweet.

WILLIAM SHAKESPEARE

The use of perfume pans to sweeten musty rooms was the 16th century equivalent of the ancient practice of burning incense to mask unpleasant odors. An alternative to the perfume pan was the French custom of using perfumed bellows.

Another practice was to spread sweet rushes, flowers or herbs on the floor, or to sprinkle rosewater on it with a casting bottle. In old England, the floors of castles, cottages and churches were usually of stone or dirt and covering them eliminated the need to sweep. It was also a good way to impress visiting dignitaries.

A young gallant in one of Marston's plays (Antonio and Mallida) enters with a casting bottle of perfumed water which he proceeds to sprinkle on himself.

In Marlowe's 'Dr. Faustus', Pride enters, saying, "Fye, what a smell is here! I'll not speak another word for a king's ransom unless the ground is perfumed."

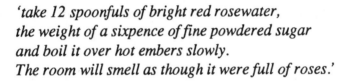

To Scent a Room

You can scent the whole house as if roses were growing indoors.

To perfume a room, try heating rosewater over hot embers as was done in King Edward VI's time:

'take 12 spoonfuls of bright red rosewater,
the weight of a sixpence of fine powdered sugar
and boil it over hot embers slowly.
The room will smell as though it were full of roses.'

You, of course, will use your stove or fireplace.

In the time of Queen Henrietta Maria, powdered cloves mixed with rosewater and placed on a hot pan 'will make a perfume of excellent good odour'.

In summer bring outdoor rose scent into your room by planting an old climbing rose, such as the almost-black flowered Guinee, near an open window. After a summer shower its fruity fragrance will be even stronger.

Lamps

Bulwer Lytton in his 'Last Days of Pompeii' refers to the burning of scented rose oil in the lamps up to the time of the catastrophe. You may not be expecting a volcanic eruption but might want to try adding a little essential rose oil to your regular lamp oil.

Light Bulbs

Put a few drops of rose oil onto light bulbs. The warmth of the bulb will suffuse the air with rose.

Floors & Doormats

When Saladin entered Jerusalem in 1167, he had the floor and walls of Omar's mosque washed with rosewater. It is still a good way to start perfuming your house.

Or, you can add a wonderful fragrance to your house by strewing fresh lavender and rose petals under your door mat. As people walk over it, crushing the plants below, the air fills with perfume.

Armchair Saddlebags

Another way to use roses and lavender (together or alone) is to fill slim miniature 'saddlebags' with these flowers and to put them on the backs of armchairs. The visitor who leans back in the chair wonders where the sweet fragrance is coming from.

Rose Potholders

Stuff your potholders with dried rose petals and other complementary herbs. When they touch a warm dish or pan the fragrance is released in the kitchen. Use rose patterned fabric. These make a great gift for brides or Aunt Mabel.

Table & Bed Linen

"Let's go to that house," says Izaak Walton, "for the linen looks white and smells of lavender, and I so long to be in a pair of sheets that smell so."

What better treat than to go off to sleep against bed linens smelling of lavender and roses. To make these sweet smelling linens, stand some bergamot and lavender petals in rosewater overnight and add to the rinse water after you have done your washing.

Or, try sprinkling some rose powder onto your sheets and pillows.

(see Powder recipe in AFTER BATH OILS AND POWDERS). As Shakespeare said:

> There will we make our bed of roses
> And a thousand fragrant posies.

Pillows

If you are not already too intoxicated with fragrance, add bed pillows stuffed with hops and rose petals to bring sweet untroubled sleep.

Herbs have been used, over the centuries, to stuff both mattresses and pillows. Sweet woodruff, lavender and roses were favorites.

Keep in mind how you will use the pillow. If they are to be used on the bed and under your head, you will want them to be soft and flat. Before chemical sedatives were readily available, people put tiny pillows filled with dried flowers and spices under their heads at night to induce sleep.

When the herbs and flowers have lost their fragrance, more can be added. The pillows should be rubbed and stroked and fluffed just before they are put to use.

Sleep Pillow

Take by weight:

3 oz. rose petals (dry)
2 oz. mint (dry)
1/2 oz. crushed cloves

Mix together and place in a small cloth bag and it will help you sleep. These little cushions, made small enough to take from room to room or when travelling, are a direct descendant of the herb stuffed mattress.

Fragrant Dreams

To the above recipe, add sweet basil.

Rose Lilac Pillow

3 parts rose petals (dry)
2 parts lilac (dry)
2 parts marjoram (dry)
Mix together.

Candles & Incense

Hundreds of years before America bestowed the fragrance of tobacco smoking upon the old world, the Europeans had discovered that burning fragrant woods and gums was so pleasurable that they not only wanted their houses filled with smoke but also their temples. People also burned incense to keep away disease and to perfume their clothing.

Smoke seemed to enhance the enchantment of fragrance, especially before the discovery of the distillation of perfumes which came early in the 10th century. Today we blend together these fragrant woods and gums with other fragrant materials to burn as incense in our homes. Incense is very easy to make, and fun to experiment with.

You can put together lovely fragrances that will add beauty to your life. The fragrance can be planned to evoke a desired mood or emotion. So, set up your 'rose lab' and make like Merlin the Magician.

Incense

The base for the following recipes is finely ground dry sawdust. Aromatic materials are added and the mixture made into a dough using a gum arabic syrup.

Basic Recipe for Molded Incense

1 cup sawdust
2 2/3 tbsp. powdered gum arabic
1 cup water

To make syrup, mix together gum arabic and water until smooth. Put sawdust in bowl and add perfumed materials. Add syrup a little at a time until mixture feels grainy and can be molded. Fondle into cylindrical shapes.

After the cylinders dry a bit so they can be handled, put toothpicks inside them to act as stems. Dry 48 hours before burning. Aging improves the fragrance. Keep in a dry closed container.

NOTE: The sawdust mixture may appear as though it will not stick together. However once you shape it, it will stay that way.

Rose Incense
1 cup sawdust
1 cup gum arabic syrup
1/4 cup gum benzoin (powdered)
1 dropper rose essential oil (or more as desired)
NOTE: One dropper is equivalent to 20 to 24 drops.

Rose Incense Mixes
For a brief but fragrant encounter, try blending the following fragrant ingredients and burning a pinch or two at a time. Store in glass jars. A jar of this, with instructions for use, makes a lovely gift.

Rose Sandalwood Mix
2 tbsp. heavily scented rose petals (powdered)
2 tbsp. sandalwood chips
2 tbsp. sawdust

Romantic Rose Mix
1 tbsp. fragrant roses
1 tbsp. patchouli leaves
2 tbsp. sawdust
1 tbsp. gum benzoin (powdered)
1 tbsp. sandalwood chips

TO USE: Make a paper cone by cutting out a paper triangle about 2 1/2 inches at the widest part. Roll it into a cone and staple at the top.

Bend a paper clip into an S shaped holder. Set the holder in a bowl of sand. Insert the cone filled with incense. Light the bottom end.

Try experimenting with your own blends.

Candles

Wherever early man hunted for honey he also found beeswax for candles. The warm light from these candles has been associated with civilization since the early Egyptians left beeswax candles in the tombs of their great men and women. In Crete, about 3000 B.C., beeswax candles were usually made in a cone shape around a reed for a wick and used to light the palace of King Minos. Beeswax with its honey-smell and its soft light was also used extensively in the very richest homes.

By Medieval times, candle making was divided between the Wax Chandlers, who made the superior wax candles by rolling beeswax into cylinders, and the Tallow Chandlers, who worked with the inferior but far more common animal fats.

By the 19th century candles were improving as new waxes were introduced, but their life as useful illumination was waning as gas and then electricity replaced them. However, despite all modern methods of illumination, candles live on to delight us. The mystery of their soft, flickering light encourages conversation.

Add candles to your incense scented room and you have set the stage for romance.

The main ingredients of candles are paraffin wax, stearic acid, and appropriate fragrances or scents.

Stearic acid may be used in quantities from five to 30 percent. As the quantity is increased, harder, longer-burning and more opaque candles are produced.

The most effective way to scent a candle is to add the essential oil or fragrance to the melted ingredients just prior to pouring the liquid mixture. One quarter of an ounce (half a tablespoon) of essential oil is sufficient to scent about three pounds of the mixture. Popular scents are rose, pine, and sandalwood.

Molds for home-made candles can be made from paper towel rolls, milk cartons, salad molds and other household containers.

Rose Scented Candle

Left-over unscented candles or paraffin wax blocks
Crushed dried rose petals
Pieces of red wax crayon for color
Ground cinnamon or other spice
Rose essential oil

Melt wax candles and crayons in container sitting in hot water. Remove from heat and stir in petals, spices and essential oil.

To make the wick, dip a string, that is several inches longer than the mold, into the wax leaving a few inches unwaxed. Remove and pull taut to straighten. Tie the unwaxed end to a long pencil or stick. Position the string down the centre of the mold and rest the pencil or stick across the top of the mold.

Pour the melted wax around the wick adding whole petals for more fragrance. Allow candle to harden before removing. Trim the wick. If you used a paper mold just tear it away. Run hot water over the outside of metal molds.

For a honey rose scent use a beeswax and paraffin mixture.

HINT: You can create a layered look by pouring a small portion of one color, letting it set to the 'rubbery' stage, then pouring another color, letting it set, and so on.

SPECIAL EFFECT: Crack walnuts carefully. Pour scented rose wax into these little half shell 'bowls' and let set. Drill a hole for a small length of wick of appropriate size. These small 'boats' can be floated in a large bowl of water for the dinner table or on a pond for an outdoor barbeque party.

Bowl of Lights
Candle stubs or paraffin
String for wicks
A flat bowl
2 small sticks slightly longer than the bowl is wide
Collection of roses and leaves

Rest the two sticks across the top of the bowl. Tie the three pieces of wick string to each stick so the ends touch the bottom of the bowl.

Melt the candle stubs in a small saucepan resting in a larger one with water in it. Heat the water slowly until wax has melted. Remove from heat and take out the wick ends with a fork.

Carefully pour shallow layer of melted wax into bowl. Scatter some leaves and flowers on top. Repeat and finish with enough wax to almost fill the bowl.

When the wax is cool and hard, cut the wicks just under the sticks with scissors.

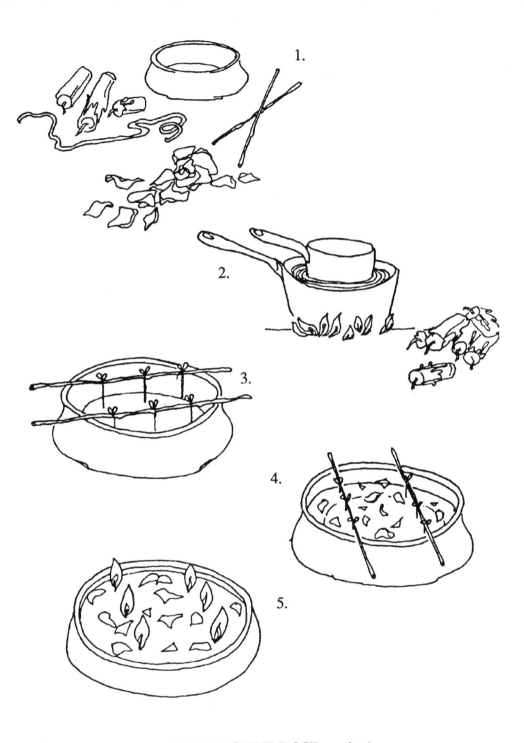

(for Pomanders, see WEARING THE ROSE section)

Essential Oils

Once it was thought that the essential oil binder of a flower, such as a rose, was a single characteristic substance. Investigation showed this is not so; that all plant oils are made up of numerous chemical ingredients including the identifying and dominant odor, plus many supplementary ones.

For instance, the basis of the odor in all fragrant roses is geraniol, a highly complex substance containing oil of lemon, oil of orange, oil of bay leaves, etc.

With such knowledge, chemists have learned to extract chemicals with similar odors from more abundant and cheaper materials such as coal tar and crude oils. Using combinations of these extractions they have built up a shelf of chemical substitutes.

In the case of the rose, no two varieties are exactly alike, and a whole range of essential oils, each subtly different, is produced. In some, like the red rose, the white rose and the Marechal Niel, the difference is so marked that it is readily detected. Even the fragrance of the same species varies according to the soil, the climate and the method of cultivation.

Such variations are being constantly studied by scientists who have been able to establish how the individual constituents of these essential oils are formed in the plant, and how the quality and quantity of yield might be improved.

Dioscordes, in the first century, gives the earliest description for making rose oil. It is a lengthy process wherein sesame oil and roses are boiled together. The oil is then pressed out with hands that have been anointed with fragrant honey, and, after each maceration the vessel containing the oil must be covered with honey.

Nowadays distillation is the method usually employed to extract scent of roses. There are two distillation methods. 1. Boiling the plant in water, as in making rosewater (see COSMETIC section). 2. Steaming or 'dry' method.

Distillation

SIMPLE STEAM METHOD

The following is a simple steam method you may want to try. You will need an enamel, glass or stainless steel kettle, a long rubber tube and ice. Pick lots of scented flowers or leaves. Use rose only, or make up your

own combinations of, say, lavender, roses and mint leaves. Put them in the kettle and just cover them with cold water (distilled water is best).

You now need a long rubber tube and a plastic bag full of ice cubes. Fit one end of the rubber tube tightly into the spout of the kettle so no steam can escape. Now, push the tube through a hole at one end of the ice bag, through the ice and out the other end of the bag. Put this end into a glass jar to catch the essence.

Gently simmer the kettle. You will see drops of essence collecting after a while. Store in tiny bottles of dark glass.

OTHER METHODS

Sometimes the high temperature of distillation destroys or damages the aromatic substances. In such cases, maceration or enfleurage can be used. Maceration is best for roses.

Maceration is the extraction of the perfume by immersion in liquid fats or oils, at a temperature of 60° or 70 °C. The petals are mixed in large pans with the hot grease or oil and continuously stirred for a specific time. This ruptures the cells containing the essential oil. The contents are then turned out onto a screen and the fat drained off. Fresh flowers are then added to the fat and the operation repeated until the desired strength is reached.

SIMPLE MACERATION METHOD

Cover the flower petals or herbs with vegetable or mineral oil, about 2 cups of oil to 1/2 cup of tightly packed flower petals. Warm the oil slightly and keep the jar in the sun or some other warm place. Keep the lid on tight. Every day strain the mixture through cheesecloth and add fresh flowers. Do this daily for at least a month.

Obviously this project is best attempted in summer when the supply of flowers is limitless. You can start with lilacs, go on to lily-of-the-valley and roses when the lilacs fade, and so on through the blooming season.

ENFLEURAGE

This technique requires the use of pure alcohol but you can substitute vodka. Make sure it is as scentless as possible.

Coat the bottom of a large glass baking dish with a thin layer of lard. Sprinkle a layer of fresh rose petals over the lard. Cover the dish tightly with a lid or aluminum foil, sealing the edges with tape. Keep in the dark overnight. The next day, pick out any wilted petals and replace with fresh ones. Seal them in. Do this every day for at least two to three weeks.

Remove all petals from the dish and set it in a pan of hot water to melt the lard. Pour the melted fat into a jar, straining to remove any bits of flowers. Add an equal amount of alcohol or vodka and seal with a tight-fitting lid. Store in a dark place for another two to three weeks - the longer the better.

During the first stage, the petals transfer their scent to the lard. During the second, the lard transfers the scent to the alcohol. When the alcohol has picked up most of the scent, pour it off into little bottles with tight stoppers. The lard that remains is called 'pomade'. Pack it in jars and use as a moisturizer.

NOTE: For larger quantities, you can layer the lard and flowers between sheets of glass, one on top of the other to a reasonable height, and seal in aluminum foil.

CAUTION: Never put essential oils in plastic containers. Use dark colored glass with lid. Essential oils can deteriorate if exposed to light, air or excessive heat.

Some Uses for Essential Oils

- As a perfume (use on pulse points, or soak piece of cotton and put in bra)
- Rub inside drawers to perfume lingerie and linen.
- A few drops add lasting aroma to potpourris and sachets.
- A few drops added to coconut or almond oil makes a good massage lotion.
- Rub on light bulb to scent room.
- See AROMATHERAPY

Potpourri

At one of his parties Nero ordered his servants to cover the whole surface of Lake Lucina with roses. And it is said when Seneca had his bed spread with roses, he could not sleep if a single petal was curled. But the taste for perfumery reached its climax in Egypt with Cleopatra. She had the floors of the palace covered with roses to a depth of 18 inches and her mattresses stuffed with them.

So faithful are the scents of roses that well prepared potpourri made from rose petals and spices will continue to give off scent for 20 years or more.

Potpourris are colorful mixtures of flowers, combined with such aromatic and fragrant materials as spices, herbs, rinds, essential oils and other materials—all bound together with a fixative, often orris root powder, which absorbs the aromatic oils and holds them for long periods of time. There are two methods of making potpourris, wet and dry.

The function of a fixative, such as orris root, is to both hold and blend other scents. Fixatives should be whole or cut for potpourris and powdered for sachets.

Rose petals are the main ingredient of potpourri. You will need about four times as many of these as other flowers. Gather them in the early morning after a rainless period of at least 24 hours. Dry as described in chapter on METHODS.

It is best to start with the most fragrant roses possible of which Damask and Gallica are two of the best. Of the latter, there is a variety known as the Apothecary's Rose (*Rosa gallica officinalis*). If these are not available choose the most highly scented roses you can find.

The balance of the potpourri mixture is important. An increase in suggested amounts can make for a confused aroma. In particular, do not be heavy-handed with any strong scents like eucalyptus or mint. A little goes a long way.

Choose a beautiful container—an apothecary jar, ceramic pot, openwork silver, china, or porcelain box. If the potpourri is to be seen, arrange it so that leaves, small rosebuds or other pretty flowers show.

Before today's atomizers, the custom of a rose jar was used to refresh and fill a room with fragrance or to disguise unpleasant odors.

WET METHOD

Potpourris in earlier times were made by the moist method where roses are salted down in a crock then mixed with other ingredients and a bit of brandy or good perfume. Placing a weight on top of the mixture helps draw out the oils.

The advocates of the moist potpourri method usually scorn the dry method, saying, truthfully, that too much of the fragrant oil in rose petals is lost by completely drying them. The object of the moist method is to dry the petals just enough so they lose only half their fragrance. Roses are about half dry when the total bulk has been reduced by one half, the petals about half their size and flabby.

Potpourri is probably a descendent of the pomander used medicinally in sick rooms and churches. The following moist method recipe is said to keep its fragrance for fifty years.

Century Fragrance
1 peck (8 quarts) partially dried rose petals
3/4 lb. sea salt
1/2 lb. finely powdered bay salt
1/2 lb. allspice
1/2 lb. brown sugar
1/4 lb. of gum benzoin
2 oz. powdered orris root
1 gill (1/2 cup) of brandy

Gather roses early in the day when perfectly dry. Pick off the petals and cover them with the salt. Cover with a plate with a weight on top. Leave them for several days and if fresh flowers are added, also add the right proportion of salt. Then mix in all the spices. Add the brandy, and, if you choose, add any other source of fragrant flowers or leaves such as lavender and verbena—but they must be perfectly dry first.

The mixture must be kept well stirred and in a covered jar. If it gets too dry it can be moistened with more brandy.

DRY METHOD
For this method roses and other flowers and leaves must be bone dry. For drying see Chapter on METHODS.

Simpler Century Fragrance
Dried rose petals
1 part fine table salt (noniodized)
1 part powdered borax (USP grade)
1/10 part powdered cinnamon

To every quart of rose petals add two teaspoons of the salt, borax, cinnamon mixture and stir once or twice a day, adding other dried flowers or leaves. You might try geranium leaves, lemon-scented verbena, lavender, sweet-scented herbs, and thyme; also add the correct proportion of salt-borax-cinnamon mixture.

Rose Jar
4 quarts dried rose petals
salt (noniodized)
3 oz. broken allspice and cinnamon stick
1 oz. each cloves, nutmeg, mace, anise seed, grated orange peel, grated
   lemon peel

In large crock place layer of dried rose petals and salt. Repeat until roses are used, ending with layer of salt. Place a heavy weighted plate, which covers the inside of the crock, over the mixture. Let stand overnight. Gently stir, being sure salt is even throughout. Do this daily for a week. Add allspice. Stir three more days. During each of these three days, add daily another 1/4 oz. broken allspice and cinnamon sticks. Now add other spices. Place in ornamental jars with tight fitting lids.

Floral Bouquet
1 quart dried rose petals
1 cup dried lavender
1 tbsp. rosemary
1 tsp. each of cloves, cinnamon and nutmeg
1 tbsp. each of gum benzoin and gum storax

Place petals and lavender in container leaving lots of room to shake the mixture. Sprinkle with gum benzoin and gum storax (if not available use orris root). Add the spices and mix together gently. Close container tightly. Shake every few days for about six weeks or until mixture is well mellowed. Then pack into pretty containers.

NOTE: You can add several drops of essential oil such as rose lavender or rose geranium. This is added last by sprinkling on top of the mixture before sealing the container. Shake as above.

Bay Rose
3 quarts dried rose petals
12 torn bay leaves
2 handsful lavender
1 handful orange blossoms, violets, carnations
   or other dried flowers of your choice
2 oz. chopped orris root
1 oz pounded nutmeg
1/4 oz. pounded cinnamon stick
1/4 oz. pounded cloves
1/2 oz. oil of neroli (or 4 tbsp. dried orange peel)
   For method see FLORAL BOUQUET recipe.

Sachets

In France in the 16th century, under Catherine de Medici, even the fountains of Paris ran with scent on great occasions. A century later another Queen of France, also a Medici, indulged extravagantly in perfumes and powders. She so 'adored' them, we are told, that she "scattered through all her chests of drawers, in all her pieces of furniture, among all her belongings, sachets of carnation taffeta filled with perfume of roses."

Queen Elizabeth's 'dry perfume' was contained in little 'bagges' that were carried in the pocket or laid among the clothes. Her favorite was Damask Powder which contained damask roses, musk, storax, labdanum, gum-benzoin, gallingal and calamus.

You can also put these little bags (sachets) in your bra or tie them around your neck with a pretty ribbon.

Sachets are different from potpourris in that they require the flowers to be finely crushed and the spices ground. Potpourri is composed of coarsely broken ingredients.

Put the sachet mixture into tiny drawstring bags or two inch square envelopes made of pretty, thin, transparent fabric trimmed with lace. Or you can use small handkerchiefs. Simply place a tablespoon or so in the centre, gather tops together and tie with a colored ribbon.

Fabrics for sachets and pillows should be chosen as carefully as the herbs which fill them. Many designs have an old-world country garden air —rose chintzes, French prints, and daintily sprigged fine cottons.

Heliotrope Sachet

8 oz. orris root
4 oz. ground rose petals and leaves
2 oz. powdered tonka beans
1 inch vanilla bean
1/2 tsp. musk essential oil (synthetic)
2 drops almond oil
Mix together. Place in bags. Tuck among towels and sheets.

NOTE: Synthetic musk, ground benzoin gum, or orris root can be used as fixatives. These agents 'fix' the scent so that it will not change with time and will prolong the life of the sachet.

Rose-Spice

1 lb. rose leaves and petals (dry)
1 oz. cloves
1 oz. caraway seeds
1 oz. allspice
4 oz. table salt (noniodized)
Grind cloves, caraway and allspice into a powder. Blend powder, rose mixture and salt. Pour into small bags for distribution among linen, shelves and drawers.

Patchouli Rose Sachet

12 cups patchouli leaves
2 handsful rose petals
2 cups sandalwood chips
3 tbsp. sandalwood powder
10 drops rose geranium oil
10 drops patchouli oil

Grind all dry ingredients together and add oils.

Marie Antoinette popularized sachets made from dried rose petals, sandalwood, cloves, coriander and lavender.

What you can do with Potpourris or Sachets
(also see THE AROMATIC HOUSEHOLD section)

- Perfume linen and clothes closets
- Place among lingerie or men's underwear and handkerchiefs
- Place among books on library shelves
- Put them in cupboards
- Carry in a pocket or purse
- Tie them to bedposts
- Slip into writing paper
- Put into folds of couches or armchairs
- Put in or under cushions
- Pin in draperies where warm sun sets fragrance free
- Stuff into hollow toilet roll holder
- or just display in an open container for beauty and fragrance.

7 Wearing the Rose

In the early 1600's both men's and women's round-toed shoes were at first tied with a small bow or small rosette; this after 1610 became a huge rose designed for display and concealing the tie underneath. The heels and the sides of the soles were colored red for full dress; this remained fashionable in the court until the 18th century.

Flame and rose colored clothing were also fashionable. The glowing velvety crimson of the damask rose is associated with active passion. Lighter shades of red from rose to the faintest shrimp-pink are related to the affections. A deep rose is the traditional color of romantic love, both sexual and emotional. As more and more white (purity, innocence) is added the sensual content diminishes.

Over the centuries floral patterns have also been very common in women's clothes. The blooms may be tiny and delicate or huge and bold to suit everyone from a Little Nell to a Carmen.

Once upon a time men wore clothes covered with floral designs. After about 1800 however, except for an occasional flowered waistcoat, this floral decoration reverted back to women.

Pink and rose lingerie, with a good deal of lace, are favored by women who think of love as romance and of themselves as romantic heroines. One can also buy underthings in floral patterns representing a delicate or a blousy femininity.

Clothing Perfumes were never richer, more elaborate or more costly than in Elizabeth I's reign. Her perfumed cloaks, the sandalwood or cedar coffers in which the royal linen and clothes were kept, the liberal use of the 'casting bottle' from which rosewater was sprinkled on the floor of her apartment—all gave her immense pleasure and set the fashion for perfume in every castle and country house.

In olden days guests were always treated with great respect. They were offered bowls of scented clay to wash away the dust of travel and a bowl of rosewater for a fragrant rinse.

Another special way to give them pleasure was to hang their clothes over a charcoal brazier which had been sprinkled with frankincense, myrrh and storax so the next time they put them on they smelled heavenly.

The Egyptian enchantress, Mythris, asked to be buried in a rose embroidered cloak and her tomb was filled with rose petals and flowers.

One Arab sultan was so obsessed with the rose that his rugs were sprinkled continuously with rose perfume and he even wore rose-pink clothes.

In Jerusalem in the 12th century when a visitor was expected to leave, the scenser was used to perfume his garments; this was a gentle hint that the guest was in danger of outstaying his welcome.

HINT: Why not rinse your undies or blouses in clear (not red) rosewater?

Toga Be as rose conscious as the Romans with an easy to make toga. Use a rose-colored or rose-patterned material.

Rose Trims The damask rose has given its name to the pale-pink color of fashion, Damask pink.

To add a Damask rose motif to your own dress try applique, crewel or embroidery. Patterns and ideas can be found in the library, craft shops or sewing departments.

Wear a rose-colored scarf tied in the shape of a rose around the neck, the waist, the head or the wrist. Or add an artificial rose to a flowing scarf.

Rose Shoe English court dress in the 17th century shows both men's and women's round-toed shoes trimmed with roses. The roses were made of ribbon, lace or leather. Red heels were often added. The woman's shoe might also have a lace ruffle.

Puritan men in the Commonwealth wore square-toed shoes for full dress. With the shoes of black leather, the square heels were painted red. Shoes were fastened by small 'roses' or flat ribbon bows.

Rose Ribbon Bow for Your Shoe A modern shoe can often be adapted to 17th century style with a ribbon rosette. Avoid extremely pointed toes; a tapered, blunt toe is best. Create the rosettes out of ribbon and back the ribbon with horsehair if a stiff shape is desired. Hat wire can be stitched or glued to the back of leather strips for the same purpose.

Scented Gloves Elizabeth wore the scented gloves so fashionable in her day. A pair was presented to her by Leicester and went by the name of Leicester's perfume.

The passion for scented gloves seems to have lasted for three centuries at least, and in France three red gloves are incorporated in the coat of arms of the perfumers.

Frangipani gloves were the craze of the 15th and 16th centuries—

the perfume invented by a Roman nobleman. The glove powder was composed of equal quantities of every obtainable spice to which was added the weight of the whole in orris root, with one percent of musk. This powder must not be confused with the frangipani we know today, which is distilled from flowers.

In the 17th century, frangipani gloves gave way to 'Neroli' gloves, distilled from orange flowers and called after the Princess of Neroli.

Rose Glove Recipe

Gently wash the gloves in warm white wine. Sprinkle with rosewater and leave to dry in the shade. After a week, scent with rose oil and rose powder blended well in a mortar. If you prefer a spicy rose scent, add a drop or two of clove or cinnamon oil.

Put a small quantity at a time on the gloves and by degrees 'chase it' with a clean hand. This will leave a rich and lasting perfume, a scent to greatly refresh the spirits.

Jewelry

The circlets and crowns worn by the Egyptians grew progressively more elaborate and ornate. From these crowns with roundels, rosettes and composite flowers evolved the crown of roses characteristic of the Isis cult in Roman times.

Rose petals garlanded the heads of the worthy Romans. Soldiers went into battle wearing wreaths of roses and the victorious chariots were bedecked with the flowers when they returned to Rome.

Among antique jewelry are perforated lockets that once contained perfume, and rings that held a few grains of dry perfume. The bezels were tiny boxes with perforated lids. Both the lockets and the rings were the 19th century successors to the cassolette and the pomander.

Amulet rings were usually worn on the third finger—the medicine finger—and meant to act as love charms or as a protection against illness.

Pomanders, Beads and Brooches

Queen Elizabeth led the fashion of carrying in the hand a pomander, a small ball composed of ambergris, benzoin and other aromatics. It is said, she was mightily pleased with the gift of a number of miniature pomanders, strung together like large beads and worn round the neck.

Originally designed to be carried to ward off infection and to subdue unpleasant odors, pomanders soon became an excuse for the creation of exquisite pieces of jewelry. Hollow gold or silver balls were created to be filled with fragrant gums and spices. They either hung from the neck or dangled from the belt, where they could be reached in a hurry.

As personal cleanliness became more commonplace, pomanders were taken off the body and changed from pieces of jewelry to room ornaments. These pomanders were often made of china, richly decorated, and they were filled with fragrant mixtures and hung around the room.

Men and women wore jewelry made of scented gums. Travelling salesmen carried these gums into the countryside where housewives shaped them into necklaces and bracelets. The gums were often mixed with herbs, honey, spices and rolled into beads or balls.

Rose beads were a favorite, girdling m'lady's waist and neck. Even after many years they retain their haunting rose fragrance.

Rose Beads
2 quarts rose petals
Rosewater
Rose oil

Grind or chop petals finely. Place in iron pot (this helps produce rich black color of the beads). Cover with rosewater and heat at low temperature for 2 to 3 hours, or until a softened mass. There should be no excess water when slightly warm pulp is ready.

Oil your palms with rose oil and roll pulp into small beads. Place on absorbent cloth or towel. To make the holes, stick beads on metal knitting needles or embroidery needles until dry. Twist occasionally to keep the needles freely moving. Remove. Thread beads.

Rosy Pomander Balls
Most of us think of pomanders as clove-studded oranges but the same lasting fragrance can be obtained, at much less cost, by using apple pulp. Wear one around your neck on a ribbon, tie one to your waist or hang them in your rooms or closets.

The following recipe makes 25 balls.
Apples to make 2 cups drained pulp

2 tsp. ground cloves

1 1/2 tsp. ground nutmeg

1 tsp. ground ginger

1 1/2 tsp. ground or powdered orris root

De-stem and core apples. Do not peel. Cook. Press the pulp to remove most of the moisture. If you wish, leave overnight, refrigerated, to drain.

To 2 cups drained pulp, stir in: cloves, nutmeg, ginger and orris root. Mix thoroughly. Shape into 1 1/2 to 2 inch balls. Roll in the following mixture until they begin to feel dry.

3 tbsp. orris root

1/2 tsp. rose oil

1/4 cup ground cinnamon

1/4 cup ground cloves

Wrap each ball in a square of porous fabric that is easily pinked with shears. Tie with ribbon and hang to dry.

Clay Rose Brooch

Lump of clay about size of a small egg

Rose extract or perfume

Poster paints and brush

1 inch brooch pin

Impact adhesive

Mix a few drops of rose extract or perfume into clay. Use your fingertips to press out a strip of clay about 6 inches long and 3/4 inches wide. The edges should be slightly uneven.

Begin rolling up the strip tightly at first to represent the centre of the rose, then more loosely to represent the outer petals. Continue rolling until the flower is complete, then pinch off the remainder of the strip.

Moisten the inner edge of the strip and press firmly against the flower to secure it. Turn the rose over, and with a moistened fingertip, flatten the back to make a smooth base.

Set the rose to dry, then paint it. If you choose, add some rose perfume to the paint. When the paint is dry, use impact adhesive to secure the brooch pin in place on the base.

Roses in the Hair

In the early 19th century women's long hair was adorned with a profusion of ornaments from full-blown roses to ostrich feathers and jewelled stars. Hair was crimped and ringletted and sometimes piled high on the head and topped with roses.

By 1850 styles were simpler but still sported ringlets, large chignons and were more likely to be trimmed with a single rose.

Among the 'upper classes', long ringlets and 'falls' were in style by 1870 with mounds of hair piled high and again trimmed with roses or ribbons.

Cosmetics

Rose oil and rosewater have been used since time immemorial—the oil for massage, the rosewater for beautifying the hands and face. No other fragrance has such universal appeal. And after a thousand years and more, it is still the custom in the Middle East to welcome a guest or a stranger with a sprinkling of rosewater from a gulabdan—a type of vase with a long tapering neck or spout ('gul' means rose).

The word 'cosmetic' comes to us from the ancient Greeks, whose word 'kosmein' meant "to decorate". The Greeks and Romans believed that the body was a temple and an object for respect. They believed in caring for their bodies through baths and exercise. In Rome, this gradually gave way to frequenting massage houses where highly scented oils were used, usually by attractive slaves of either sex.

Some cosmetics began as a real need. For example the ancient Egyptians used the oil of the castor bean to protect themselves from the desert sun.

In the Middle Ages there were continual conflicts between the populace who used cosmetics for quite practical reasons and the church who condemned their use. At that time, with bathing at an all-time low, the use of perfumed rosewater was an urgent necessity.

In the 1500's and 1600's the use of scents of different kinds increased. Clothing was scented—in England most often with lavender and on the Continent with roses. About this time affluent English women began to apply cosmetics habitually. Queen Elizabeth I, who used cosmetics generously, established the custom among all classes.

In the 1700's cosmetics began to find a wider acceptance among both men and women in Europe. Perfume shops began to appear and rouge made its debut. The French, both men and women, used cosmetics far more than the English—rouge, face and breast powder, hair oils and pomades and flower waters.

Today we totally accept the use of cosmetics.

Rosewater

Roses—man's favorite flower.

Shakespeare refers to the rose in no fewer than 14 of his plays. In the Taming of the Shrew he refers to the use of rosewater for perfuming the hands:

> *What is it your honour will command*
> *Let one attend him with a silver basin*
> *Full of rosewater, and bestrew'd with flowers.*

Rosewater was prepared as early as the 10th century. In England, in the 16th century, the first Queen Elizabeth had a still-room at Hawkshead where the ladies of the court amused themselves in distilling fragrant waters. In the houses of the nobility, the still-room was as important as the kitchen.

So precious were roses in France at that time that ordinary inhabitants were prohibited from cultivating them. Roses were often included in manorial rights. The lord of the manor levied a tax of so many bushels of rose petals to make rosewater for his household.

Rosewater is wonderful for the skin—be it as an aid to wrinkles and dryness, puffiness, eczema, or large pores. It is the main ingredient in many rose recipes.

To make rosewater you can use fresh or dried petals. You can dry your own or they can be purchased from most herbal outlets. In recipes, you use more of the fresh petals than the dried petals.

Rosewater can be used alone to refresh the skin. Or, you can mix equal parts rosewater and vinegar. This rose vinegar can be used to adjust the pH level of your skin before applying a moisturizer. It can also be used as a deodorant by saturating a cotton ball, and as a refreshing body rub.

Dried Rose Petals

2 cups dried rose petals
4 cups water

Simmer one cup petals in four cups hot water in covered pot for 45 minutes. Strain, pressing with spoon to get out all essence. Mix in another cup petals, heat as before. Strain. Bottle. Preserve in refrigerator.

Fresh Rose Petals

2 parts petals
1 part hot water

Blend well in blender, simmer 15 minutes. Repeat until you get strength desired.

Rose Vinegar

Mix equal parts rosewater and vinegar.

NOTE: Always use glass, enamel or stainless steel equipment.

Rose Facial Creams

One of the most highly recommended homemade creams known to our grandmothers was Creme Marquis. It contained both rosewater and attar of roses. However, attar of roses is very expensive. It takes 60,000 roses to produce one ounce of attar.

Since most of us are not Oriental potentates, we cannot afford attar of roses but can afford to make homemade creams using rosewater and rose essential oils.

Rosewater has been an essential ingredient in cosmetics for centuries. It is very refreshing to the skin and is good for all skin problems. The creams make your skin soft and smooth and the scent is wonderful. Around the world, rose is the favorite scent of both sexes.

Every woman should be familiar with the name of Galen because he invented cold cream nearly two thousand years ago. It contained almond oil and rosewater and today is prepared very much as it was then. It is still one of the best beauty creams.

The following Old-fashioned Cold Cream recipe is based on Galen's 2000 year old recipe except we've replaced the white beeswax with lanolin which comes from the wool of sheep. Lanolin is very similar to the sebum or oil in human skin.

Pamper yourself with rose creams. They will do wonders for both your body and your self-esteem.

Easy Cold Cream

Skin cream of your choice
2 oz. warmed rosewater
1/8 tsp. borax (USP grade)

Put cream in blender. Slowly add rosewater into which borax has been mixed.

Different skin creams will absorb different amounts of water. Add until cream is of consistency of your choice.

Old-fashioned Rose Skin Cream

2 tbsp. aloe vera gel
3 oz. almond oil
1 oz. lanolin
2 oz. rosewater (warmed)
1/8 tsp. USP borax
rose essential oil or perfume (optional)

In blender, mix aloe vera and almond oil. Pour into top of double boiler and melt in lanolin over hot water. Remove from heat. Slowly add warmed rosewater (to which borax has been added) while beating at medium speed until cool. If desired, add several drops essential rose oil or perfume. Spoon into jar. Keep refrigerated.

Use as a body cream, as a night-time moisturizer, and for healing pimples.

Cocoa-Rose Neck Smoother

1 tbsp. cocoa butter
1 tbsp. lanolin
1/2 cup wheat germ oil or corn oil or peanut oil
4 tbsp. rosewater (warmed)
1/8 tsp. USP grade borax (approx)

Melt all three oils in double boiler until dissolved. Slowly blend in warmed rosewater to which borax has been added. Cool, place in jars and refrigerate.

Lanolin, Almond Oil and Borax can be purchased at a drug store.

If you do not wish to keep your creams in the refrigerator, a suggested preservative is Methyl Paraben.

Rose Lotions

If Elizabeth I had a favorite among flowers it was undoubtedly the rose. Attar of roses had not yet been discovered, nor was alcohol known as a solvent.

Damask rosewater and rosewater were the chief perfumes of the day; grains of musk were added to give damask water its musty odor. Today musk is astronomically priced so if you choose to add musk to a recipe you will likely have to substitute a synthetic.

Roses impart a heavenly fragrance to any preparation; they add a touch of luxury. Soak eight ounces of rosebuds and petals in enough oil to thoroughly moisten them; then use the oil as a lovely moisturizer. Or, simmer rose petals in honey to release their essence and use as a moisturizer.

The following preparations all contain rosewater. They make wonderful gifts and are sure to be appreciated by the lucky recipient.

Comfort Lotion

2 oz. rosewater
1/2 oz. extra heavy mineral oil
1/2 tsp. lanolin (dissolve over hot water)
Shake well. Rub into hands and feet to prevent roughness.

Astringent Face Lotion

1 part rosewater
2 parts witch hazel
Shake together.

Tightens and refreshes skin. Use to clean and freshen make-up midday. This is also a great after-shave lotion for the man in your life. Especially good for oily skin.

Chapped Skin Lotion

1 part rosewater
1 part glycerine
Put in small bottle and shake well before using.

Terrific Oatmeal Lotion

3 tbsp. oatmeal
1/2 cup rosewater

Grind oatmeal to powder in blender. Add rosewater. Whirl to milky fluid. Strain through gauze.

Refrigerate and shake well before using daily. Rinse off before applying make-up. Result—silky smooth skin.

Luxury Lotion

1/2 cup rosewater
1 tsp. honey
1/2 tsp. lemon juice
Blend together. Refrigerate and use daily.

Great after a good facial cleansing. Rinse well. Blot dry. Gently massage in this rose/honey lotion. A real pick-me-up at any time of day.

If you do not wish to keep your lotions in the refrigerator, a suggested preservative is Methyl Paraben.

Facial Saunas

Herbs and flowers will only yield their essential oils when subjected to heat, so those rich in fragrant oils are especially effective when used in a facial sauna. Try a sauna whenever your skin feels clogged or looks dull and is a poor color.

Saunas stimulate the action of the pores and are an effective way to deep cleanse and soften the skin. They help with the removal of blackheads and are also good for those suffering from acne and large pores.

Scented roses can be used alone or with herbs such as lavender. The Romans threw lavender into their baths not only to scent the water but to act as a disinfectant.

For a healing facial sauna try a mixture of comfrey and roses, or marigold and roses.

During a facial sauna you also benefit from inhaling the aromatic vapors. A certain quantity of odiferous molecules penetrate the skin; others stimulate the nerve endings of the olfactory organ in the nose. These nerve endings are responsible for, among other things, governing our feelings of pleasure, contentment and well-being.

Take 15 for Yourself

For a complete cleansing and stimulation of the facial skin, steam your face weekly.

Boil two quarts of water. Add two tablespoons of fresh or dried rose petals or rose-herb mixture. Let boil for five minutes, then pour into a bowl. Lower your head over the bowl and drape a large towel over you and the bowl. The steam will penetrate and cleanse your pores.

Continue the bath for five to ten minutes, then rinse your face with very cold water to close the pores. Afterward, apply a freshener for dry or normal skin; an astringent for oily skin.

There are fairly inexpensive commercial saunas, scientifically controlled for sensitive skins to reach a gentle 118°F. The result is the same: as the skin perspires, oil and makeup loosen, pores unplug. Clean skin!

Rosemary Rose Sauna

Steep a handful of rosemary and half a handful of roses in water that has been brought to a boil. Large pores are minimized, blackheads removed. This is great for teen-age or adult acne.

Clove & Eucalyptus Oil Sauna

2 tsp. oil of rose
2 tsp. oil of cloves
2 tsp. oil of eucalyptus

Combine in fast boiling water, then steam face. This sauna, due to the oily consistency of the ingredients, is good for dry, sensitive skins.

Fragrant Additives

Besides the above, use some of the following in your rose-herb mixture: Chamomile, thyme, linden blossom, mint, pine needles, camphor, or try menthol for its purgative qualities.

Facial Cleansers & Clay Masks

In the 17th century in London—from London Bridge to Whitehall —handbills flourished, many couched in the most extravagant language making fantastic claims regarding cosmetics.

There was, for example, the bill of a self-styled 'Gentlewoman' who dwelt in Surrey Street, off the Strand. There was no street numbering in those days so her address is further clarified as being "at the corner House with a White Balcony and Blue Flower-pots." In her handbill one of the items she commends is a 'miracle' face cleanser.

> *Her most excellent Wash to Beautifie the Face;*
> *also cures all Redness, Flushings and Pimples.*
> *Takes off any yellowness, morphew, sun-burn spots*
> *on the skin, and takes away the wrincles and driness*
> *caused so often by mercurial poysonous washes;*
> *rendering the worst of faces fair and tender, and*
> *preserve 'em so. You may have it from a half a crown*
> *to a Five pound a bottle.*

Well, we won't make any such extravagant promises but we will say that you will love the fragrant almond rose paste make-up remover and cleanser and delight in its lasting scent. It is a luxury item you can prepare yourself— simple and beautiful. It does lovely things to your complexion. Be lavish with the rosewater when using this recipe.

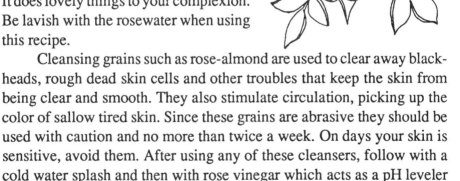

Cleansing grains such as rose-almond are used to clear away blackheads, rough dead skin cells and other troubles that keep the skin from being clear and smooth. They also stimulate circulation, picking up the color of sallow tired skin. Since these grains are abrasive they should be used with caution and no more than twice a week. On days your skin is sensitive, avoid them. After using any of these cleansers, follow with a cold water splash and then with rose vinegar which acts as a pH leveler and astringent.

Clay is a 'living' cosmetic, rich in minerals. It contains silica, iron, magnesium, calcium, sodium and potassium. When you apply a moist paste of nature's richest earth to your skin, the drying clay draws wastes and impurities from the skin and brings your blood to the surface to clean, nourish and revitalize.

Almond Rose Complexion Paste

1/2 cup blanched almonds
Rosewater

Grind almonds to fine powder in blender. Beat in enough rosewater to create a very thick paste. Pack in small clean cosmetic jars. Cover. Label and refrigerate.

TO USE: rub a small amount onto water-splashed face and rub in well. Rinse and dry.

For a longer lasting effect, rub a small amount into clean, dry face. Allow to dry completely. Brush away any particles clinging to the skin. Leave on as long as convenient. This is delightful just before retiring.

Rose Oatmeal Grains

3 parts dry oatmeal
1 part ground dried rose petals
water

Mix oatmeal and petals with water. Rub into skin, especially in areas where blackheads tend to collect. Let dry. Gently rub the mixture off with a terry washcloth and cool water. This mixture blots skin oils, as well as removing blackheads.

HINT: You can mix the dry oatmeal with rosewater.

Rose & Honey Grains

1 tbsp. corn meal
1 tbsp. ground dried rose petals
1 tbsp. (or more) honey

Gently massage to remove blackheads and rough skin. Rub the mixture off with a terry washcloth; rinse with warm, then cool, water.

Clay Facial

Add enough water to the clay to make a soft paste or a thick cream. Remember not to use metal containers or tools.

Different clays absorb different amounts of liquid but a half and half mixture is a good starting point. If the paste is too thin let it stand. Water will collect on the top and you can pour it off when the consistency is right for you.

TO USE:

Apply clay paste to freshly washed face. Spread on smoothly, leaving a wide circle around the delicate eye area. Avoid moving your facial muscles or speaking until the mask is dry. Remove with warm water, splash with cool. Blot dry.

Fennel Facial Mask

2 tbsp. Fuller's earth
2 tbsp. Okanagan clay (or other)
1 tsp. honey
1 tbsp. ground fennel
1 tbsp. ground rose petals

Mix together with enough hot water to make a loose paste. Apply to freshly washed or steamed face. Leave on 15 minutes. Rinse.

Yogurt can be used in place of water. So can glycerin.

This mask is antiseptic (medicates pores), soothing, toning, and helps remove wrinkles.

CLAY MASK VARIATIONS

1. *Dry Skin*: mix in one tbsp. of oil for each tbsp. of clay powder. Your mask will be less absorbant but will still stimulate and cleanse. Add one or two drops of rose essential oil for a delightful fragrance.
2. *Oily Skin*: boost the natural absorbancy of clay by adding rosewater. What could be more luscious than relaxing in this rose-scented bower.
3. *Sensitive Skin*: mix clay and rosewater to a custard consistency and add a teaspoon of honey. Or add a dash of wheatgerm oil for a satiny sensuous touch.
4. *New pale "Romantic Look"*: add yogurt and honey to the clay powder for a mild, natural bleaching action. Use enough rosewater to create a smooth flowing paste of medium consistency.

Bath Mystique

The Romans learnt about perfumes from the Greeks when they conquered them. As time went on they indulged more and more in the extravagant use of perfumes in their public baths which surpassed in luxury those of the Greeks.

We are told Cleopatra took sixty-nine baths a day in asses milk and that many of her voyages entailed a huge entourage of these animals and their keepers. How she ever found time for such a daily indulgence is anybody's guess.

If you are a milk bath advocate (it does give a satiny feeling once the skin is dry), you don't need asses milk. Just pour in a cupful of powdered milk plus a few drops of rose oil. Towel yourself dry without rinsing. And Hello, Cleopatra!

Bathing today is such a popular form of entertainment that a whole mystique has been built up around it. There are hundreds of bath products, all of them designed to make the entertainment more spectacular. There are oils, gellees, creams, special sponges and scrubbers, splashes and milks. Fortunately we can make a great many of these items.

Bath products can make beautiful gifts, especially if interestingly packaged. Recruit a used wine or perfume bottle, a pickle or steak sauce bottle or a cigar humidor. If you make up bath sachets use rose-patterned fabric; then the bather knows he is in for a rosy treat. Bathing in a tub of rose scented water, can be almost a mystical experience.

Whatever rose petal recipes you choose to increase the benefits of a bath, look upon them as a way of adding more comfort, beauty, and pleasure to your life.

Roses in The Bath

There are two methods for using roses in your bath:

METHOD NUMBER ONE: USING SACHETS

Mix roses and other herbs. Tie in square of cloth (5 x 5") or put in drawstring bag. Hang over faucet for hot water to run through or drop directly into tub.

METHOD NUMBER TWO: USING ROSE TEA

Mix roses, other herbs. Simmer 5 minutes. Steep 10 minutes. Pour into tub through strainer. This method is more satisfactory than Method One, as 'tea' is stronger, does a better job and the fragrance of the simmering tea is a beautiful bonus.

Rose Bath Sachet

1 oz. rose buds and petals
1 oz. peppermint or rosemary leaves
2 cups Borax, USP grade

Combine. Put 2 tbsp. in a small bag or tied in a square of cloth. Float in bath as it fills.

HINT: Add 2 tbsp. ground oatmeal or cornmeal per bag. Rub all over body before getting out for rose-petal soft skin.

Spring Tonic Sachet

1 part rose petals and/or buds
1 part orange peel (chopped in blender)

Mix. Put 2 tbsp. in cloth squares or bags. Float in bath or hang over hot water faucet.

HINT: Add 2 tbsp. ground oatmeal or cornmeal to soften skin.

Rose Bath Potpourri

1 cup cornstarch
1 cup salt
1 cup Borax, USP grade
1 cup ground dried rose petals
2 handsful whole rose petals (if desired)
1 tbsp. orris root powder (optional)
1/16 oz. rose oil

Combine ingredients except rose oil. Once mixed, blend in rose oil. Store in sealed glass container for two weeks. Use 3 tbsp. or more in small bag. Throw in tub or let hot water run through it.

Oatmeal Beauty Scrub

4 oz. almonds
4 small hotel size soaps
1/8 oz. rose oil
1 small box oatmeal

Combine almonds and soap in blender. Pulverize. Add to oatmeal. Mix in oil. Store in glass container to use for scrubs. Put 3 tbsp. in drawstring bag. After use, residue can be dumped and bag rinsed for next use.

This scrub will stimulate circulation, tone and clean.

Muscle Soothing Bath

1/2 cup bay leaves
1 cup water
1 cup rosewater

Simmer 1 cup water and bay leaves for 5 minutes. Steep for 10 minutes. Add rosewater. Strain directly into bath.

The leaves of the bay plant have always been a remedy for tired muscles.

Bath Salts & Oils

The Romans made a fetish of bathing right up until the 5th century when they were defeated by the Goths. Then came a time of the great unwashed; for one thousand years dirt and filth reigned, backed up by the religious belief that the unwashed state was a proper mortification of the flesh! St. Jerome stated, "A clean body and a clean dress mean an unclean soul".

Said a historian about medieval days "....under their chain mail the knights were scrofulous, and thick with grime and antique sweat."

Even in the 16th Century, Queen Elizabeth, according to a chronicler of the times, bathed once a month "whether she needed it or not". Queen Isabella of Spain boasted she had only two baths in her life—one when she was born and one when she was married.

On the other hand, Josephine Bonaparte luxuriated in her slipper-shaped tub which still retains the scent of her favorite perfume and sits in her dressing room at Malmaison, her chateau in Paris. The tub was presented to her by Napoleon, who had his own portable tub lugged along on his campaigns.

Today, thanks to Louis Pasteur who discovered the relationship between disease and uncleanliness, we are as clean as the Romans.

We take sensual baths, stimulating baths, medicinal baths. There are baths to absorb oiliness from your skin, others to restore oil to your skin.

Adding a handful of bath salts can turn a routine bath into a luxurious experience. The soda base of the salts neutralizes the acids secreted by the skin so that the perfume clings to the body afterwards.

A bubble bath feels plain elegant, while a baking soda bath can soothe irritated or dry skin on a sweltering hot day.

Bubble Bath Oil

1/2 cup castor or sesame or peanut oil
2 tbsp. liquid shampoo
1/2 tsp. rose oil

Beat in blender on low speed. For a spicy rose fragrance, add a few drops of oil of clove. This bath oil will keep indefinitely in a closed bottle. Shake well before using. One teaspoon per bath is sufficient.

NOTE: Castor oil is one of few oils that will disperse completely in water and not leave a ring around the tub. Also, you can substitute a nonalkaline detergent, which will not dry your skin, for the liquid shampoo in this recipe.

By-the-Sea Salts

(Lovely pink color with heady fragrance)
2 cups table salt
3 droppers rose oil
3 droppers musk (synthetic)
20 drops red food coloring

Place salt in jar. Add other ingredients. Shake well. Experiment with colors and scents.

Soda Salts

5 oz. bicarbonate of soda
3 oz. Orris root
rose oil

Mix soda and Orris root. Add several drops of rose oil, pounding in a mortar and pestle. Stored in an airtight jar, this will keep three months.

Sensual Bath Oil

7 oz. almond oil
1 oz. lecithin
1 1/2 ounces witch hazel
8 oz. rosewater

Put into bottle and shake well. Apply to wet skin and sink into bath. The water will turn the cream into a smooth-as-silk liquid that remains on the skin even after you have towelled yourself.

ALTERNATE: Try a rose/mint mixture. Simmer a handful of mint leaves in a cup of water for three minutes. Strain. Use half rosewater and half mint water in recipe.

After Bath Oils & Powders

In India the Emperor Akbar was devoted to many kind of perfumes which he mixed himself. All sweet smelling flowers were steeped in sesame oil and the scented oil used to anoint the skin and hair. Sesame oil was chosen because of its viscid quality which received the odor better. Even as late as the 16th century, this primitive method was used in India in the palaces of the great moguls and is probably much older than distillation.

Many of the Roman perfumes were made in the form of unguents, and especially those used in the baths where the anointing and perfumery of the body was one of the most important rites.

Such after-bath pampering is just as popular today. Some prefer oily products that seal water in more completely, others prefer the feeling of lighter weight more elegant moisturizers or powders. Because powder absorbs excess moisture, it soothes when rubbed into wrinkles and crevices. It is relatively easy to make rose-scented powders and softeners. They can be used any time, but are especially effective after bathing.

Easy Scented Talcum

A simple way to get a rose-scented talcum powder is to buy a large economy size commercial powder with as little scent as possible. Empty the contents into a clean glass jar and add your favorite rose cologne.

A pint-sized container of powder takes approximately four to six droppers of cologne. Shake the mixture several times a day to keep it from caking. Rose essential oil can be added in the same way. Experiment to see how much scent you want.

Bawdy Oil!

Roses — the flower of love! They are said to be a sexual stimulant for women, and may help those who complain of frigidity.

For those 'special occasions' make a body oil by adding 3 to 6 drops of rose essential oil to 3 to 4 tsp. of almond oil and then go for it!

Rose Dusting Powder

Cornstarch
Rose oil

Rub small amount of rose oil into small amount cornstarch. Gradually add more cornstarch until you have thoroughly rubbed in the rose oil. Keep the powder and a puff in a covered bowl in your bathroom.

NOTE: This is a fragrant, silky dusting powder. Cornstarch is a good base for perfumed oils. Or, you can use two parts cornstarch and one part rice flour for a grainier texture.

Creamy Softener

1/2 cup coconut oil
4 tbsp. almond oil
2 droppers rose oil

Blend and transfer to a jar with a screw cap. Coconut oil provides a barrier against cold or wind. Use before going outside.

Glycerine Softener

4 oz. glycerine
8 drops oil lavender
12 drops rose oil

Shake thoroughly. Glycerine is easy to obtain and is one of the best ingredients for chapped, roughened skin. Slick and heavy, it takes time to rub into the skin but it's worth it.

Rosewater Softener

1 part rosewater
1 part glycerine

Shake together. This has an old-fashioned fragrance.

Massage Oils & Creams

Treating the body to massage is a time-honored technique, and it is especially effective when the essential oils of flowers and herbs are used singly or in combination. Massage invigorates, strengthens, and increases circulation within the body. The internal organs, joints, even the bones, are stimulated.

The Greek physician, Hippocrates, father of medicine, said: "The way to health is to have an aromatic bath and scented massage every day."

Massage is a Chinese invention. Chinese massage, also known as acupressure, concentrates on the nerve centres and acupuncture points of the body without the use of needles. Western or Swedish massage, which most are more familiar with, is the kneading, pressing, rubbing style commonly seen in health clubs and spas.

The Greeks made a practice of massaging their bodies with aromatized oils. Epicurus went further and used a different kind of scent for each organ. In imitation of them, one eminent Scots metaphysician and lawyer of the 18th century, Lord Monboddo, smeared his body every night with a lotion of olive oil, rosewater and Venetian soap mixed with aromatic spirits.

The sedative quality of scented oils, such as rose, massaged into the skin not only relieves mental turmoil and relaxes tight muscles but effectively helps the skin carry on its primary duties of absorption, elimination and protection from the elements, in addition to being a barrier to bacteria.

The Romans, copying the Greeks, indulged more and more in the extravagant use of perfumes. In their magnificent public baths, the walls of the unctuarium or ointment rooms were lined with pots containing every kind of odoriferous unguent and essence. Their perfumes were of three kinds: 1. hedysmata: solid 2. stymmata: liquid (like our essential oils of today) 3. diapesmata: scented powders.

Resin and gum were used to fix the solid unguents and the oils were sprinkled with salt to retain their properties.

The Romans also copied many of the Greek scents, especially Cyprus, mendes and rose oil. Cyprus was used to turn other unguents green. Mendes turned them black. Myrrh dyed them blue. Rose oil had a bleaching effect.

While massage is not exactly a do-it-yourself therapy, you can, on your own, reduce bulges in areas such as the thighs, calves, hips, abdomen and arms. The trick is to stick with it until the problem is resolved.

Massage Oil
1 1/2 tbsp. lanolin
1 cup olive oil
1 dropper rose oil

Melt the lanolin over hot water and remove from heat. Warm olive oil, and mix well into melted lanolin. Add rose oil.

Irish Rose Massage Cream

1 tbsp. Irish moss (available from brewers supply)
11/4 cups rosewater
1/4 cup glycerin
1/2 tsp. boracic acid
few drops rose oil

Dissolve glycerin and boracic acid in two tbsp. rosewater. Boil Irish moss gently in remaining rosewater to form a mucilage. Combine the two mixtures. Cool and add the rose oil.

Perfumed Body Oil

2 tbsp. sunflower oil
1 tbsp. sesame oil
1 tbsp. coconut oil
1/2 tsp. liquid lecithin
1/2 tsp. lanolin
FRAGRANCE:
1 1/2 tsp. rose extract
1/2 tsp. rum extract
1/2 tsp. apricot extract
1/2 tsp. anise extract
1/4 tsp. peppermint extract

Warm the first five ingredients together. Stir until clear. Remove from heat and allow to cool. Add fragrance ingredients. Pour into an elegant bottle and shake until an opaque emulsion forms. You may need to shake it once or twice again before using.

Oil of Roses

1/2 lb. rosebuds
1 quart olive oil

Crush rosebuds fine (use mortar and pestle or blender). Put in earthenware crock and add olive oil. Place crock in sunny location for three to four weeks, stirring daily. Heat this 'sun' oil in an enamel pan until warm. Force mixture through a fine sieve or put in blender. Filter through four layers of cheesecloth and store in two ounce size, dark glass bottles.

NOTE: A simpler method for making oil of roses is to put 1/2 tsp. rose essential oil in four ounces almond oil. Shake before using.

Perfumes & Colognes

We still say: "Wake up and smell the roses!"

Throughout history the rose has been the perfume of kings and pharaohs. Cleopatra so believed in its romantic powers that when she invited Mark Anthony to her palace, she had the floors covered knee-deep in roses. The rest is history.

Scent-making became a fine art in Rome, and the scent shops occupied a whole quarter of the town. These perfume shops, called 'myropolia', became the fashionable meeting places, rather like the 18th century coffee shops.

Rose oil was added to nearly every perfume, as it is today, to tone down the heavier ingredients, and always put in last so that its scent predominated.

Sir Francis Bacon commented on how the musk rose gives off its perfume without the need to place it near the nose. A single plant set near an open window will perfume the largest of rooms.

Besides the Damask rose, both the musk rose and the old cabbage rose are grown for attar of roses; 12,000 pounds of rose petals are required to produce a pound of rose essence. The rose and orange blossom are among the few flowers which may be brought to the boil without losing their perfume.

In the early 18th century, it was the happy combination of Florentine iris, bergamot and rose which produced the famous Ess bouquet. This perfume, so admired in France, was invented in 1710 by an Englishman called Bayley who sold it at the 'Sign of the Old Civet Cat'. George IV used it at all the state balls.

Perfume is mentioned in the Old Testament, where it often takes the form of incense. The word 'perfume' is a combination of two Latin words: 'per' which means 'through' and 'fumus' which is 'smoke'. The Three Wise Men, remember, brought perfume—frankincense and myrrh—to the Christ Child.

Theophrastus (whose book on scents was written more than 200 years before the birth of Christ) tells us that in his day rose perfume was made by first steeping the roses in sweet wine. Then, along with other ingredients, a large amount of salt was added, "23 gallons of salt to 8 1/2 gallons of perfume". The use of this apparently wasteful amount of salt was peculiar only to making rose perfume.

Over the ages, many tried to 'harmonize' scents. Septimus Piesse regarded camphor, lemon, jasmine, almond, clove, sandal and rose as the seven primary odors and went so far as to prepare fifty scents, making each odor correspond with a semi note in the musical scale.

An earlier attempt to harmonize scents was made by a Breton peasant who came to Paris to give a concert of perfumes—but was regarded as a lunatic.

Lighter and more diluted than perfume are cologne and toilet water, which contain a much higher percentage of alcohol and water.

Rose Petal Oil Perfume

Pick rose petals and put them in a combination of olive oil and salt. Allow this mixture to sit in the sun for 10 days. Then filter off the liquid and store in a dark place from 6 to 8 weeks. Add a small amount of powdered orris root as a 'fixer' to make the fragrance last. The oil will be fragrant enough to be useful as a heady rub.

More complex scents can be obtained by experimenting with various flower petals and spices.

Scent of Roses

1 cup ethyl alcohol (vodka)
1/4 cup rosewater
1 tbsp. rosemary oil
2 tbsp. rose oil
1 tbsp. storax oil (fixative)

Combine in glass bottle. Shake well. Then wait four weeks to allow the fragrance to blend and fix.

Rose Cream Sachet

1/4 cup beeswax, lightly packed
1/4 cup sweet almond oil
2 tbsp. rosewater
8 droppers of rose cologne

Melt the wax in a double boiler over hot water. Using a wire whisk or electric beater, mix in olive oil until wax and oil are blended. Continuing to mix, pour in the rosewater, then remove from heat and add the cologne. Mix until thoroughly blended and pour while still warm into small containers.

This is a nice perfume to take on a trip. It won't spill.

Rose Room Cologne
2 cups fresh rose petals
2 cups alcohol (vodka)
6 tbsp. fresh lemon peel
6 tbsp. fresh lime peel
6 tbsp. fresh orange peel
1/4 cup dried basil
1/4 cup dried rosemary
1/4 cup dried peppermint leaves.

Soak the petals for one week in the alcohol in a tightly lidded jar.

The day before the week is up, grate citron peel and put in pan with the herbs; cover with boiling water and put a lid on this mixture. The next day, strain both solutions and put together in a jar, shaking well.

HINT: The Greeks were the first to appreciate the aesthetic appeal of tinted perfume. They used the root of alkanet and khroma to color their perfumes a delicate rose-pink.

Hand Smoothers & Soothers

It was from the Egyptians that the Jews learned the art of scent making. Today they use frankincense to smear their hands.

The skin on our hands has fewer natural oil cells than the skin on our faces and necks; therefore, constant moisturizing is necessary.

The great actress Sarah Bernhardt did amazing things, like sleeping in a coffin that travelled with her. What most people probably don't know is that when she stretched her hands out in a gesture of great drama, those hands had been buttered to the finger tips. Her favorite hand lotion contained no less than a pound of fresh butter.

Butter contains animal fat. Margarine contains vegetable oil. Both are good lubricants for the hands as is petroleum jelly (Vaseline).

Clay is good for soothing and cleansing your whole body. On a small scale, try a clay bath on your hands or feet. In Europe especially, sufferers from rheumatism acclaim the healing powers of Mother Earth herself.

For soothing and smoothing hands that have been working too hard, try a commercial clay soap or make our Rose Clay Hand Smoother.

Rose Clay Hand Smoother

1 tbsp. honey
1 tbsp. almond oil
1 tbsp. finely ground dried rose petals
clay powder

Beat almond oil and honey vigorously until blended. Add enough clay powder to bind. Continue beating and adding clay until you have a mixture your beater can hardly budge. Keep the cleanser in a covered glass container and pinch off a piece when you need it.

To use, moisten cleanser in cupped palms with warm water. Rub into 'lather' then wash under running warm water enough to melt oil and cool your hands with honey. Blot dry, savoring the velvety smoothness and delicious fragrance of your hands.

Special Rose Hand Cream

Our special rose hand cream can protect your hands against tomorrows' onslaughts. For this rosewater delight, melt together in a non-metallic container, over hot water:

2 tsp. grated white beeswax
1/2 cup almond oil

When melted, beat in a little at a time:

1/2 cup warmed rosewater
1/2 tsp. honey
few drops essential oil of rose

Beat until cool and pour into container. If you choose to give this cream as a delightful gift, it will make two small jars.

Satisfactory Emergency Hand Lotion

1 oz. vegetable oil
1/4 oz. honey
few drops of rose oil

Blend ingredients. Rub into the hands and give them a quick rinse under hot water. Blot dry.

Adding powdered almonds to a hand cream gives you a protective soothing coating. Keep your hand cream near the sink and use each time you wash your hands and before going out.

Oatmeal Lotion

1 cup oatmeal
1 tsp. olive oil
rosewater

Oatmeal lotion adds a layer of velvet to detergent-tormented hands. Simmer old-fashioned oatmeal (not instant variety) in enough rosewater to make a thin gruel. Strain into a container and add oil. Keep beside your sink. After washing your hands pour a small amount into your palms without rinsing off. An excellent way to overcome roughened hands.

The Glove Treatment

In the last century, women were as likely to wear gloves filled with lotion as they were to take hot water bottles to bed. If your hands are seriously ravaged try gloves. Pamper your hands with Rose Butter even while you sleep

Rose Butter

1/2 stick softened sweet butter
1 tbsp. rosewater
1 tsp. honey
ground powdered oatmeal

Beat rosewater and honey into softened butter. Beat in enough finely ground powdered oatmeal to produce a soft cream. Coat hands generously. Pull on cotton gloves and let soak in overnight.

Foot Creams, Powders & Soaks

Athenaeus, the Greek grammarian and author of 'Deipnosophistai' (the Gastronomers), tells us that some aphrodisiacs were of such strength that if applied to the soles of the feet, they immediately increased the ardor of some or calmed the fire of others.

Even the tattered old cynic, Diogenes, left his tub at the door to buy perfume—for his feet. To those who mocked him he replied: "When you anoint your head with perfume it flies away into the air and the birds only get the benefit of it; whilst if I rub it on my lower limbs it envelops my whole body and gratefully ascends to my nose."

The flexible foot is the willing workhorse of the body. Over an average lifetime of 70 years, the feet transport the body some 25,000 miles —or 2 1/2 times the circumference of the earth!

Mme. Vestris, a Victorian lady known for her beautiful feet, had her boots sewn on every morning and ripped off every night. It's said that she made more conquests with her feet than with her face. Mme. de Pompadour's two feet fitted into Louis XV's one hand.

Today our feet are much larger; not only is there more to see, but more to hurt. Besides wearing shoes that fit you, try pampering your feet with roses. Rubbing them once a week with warm, rose-scented olive oil is an excellent treat.

If you don't wear stockings in the summer time, then by all means powder the bottom of your feet with our Easy Scented Talcum (see AFTER BATH OILS AND POWDERS section). This powder can also be made using one ounce of powdered Orris to six ounces of talcum. If your feet perspire, add some powdered alum to the recipe.

In India people powder their feet with henna to keep them cool.

Super Rose Foot Rub

This will make all twenty-six of your foot bones feel pampered.
Prepare this recipe for a friend or lover.
2 drops oil of clove
4 drops oil of rose
3 tbsp. sesame oil

It makes feet smell like freshly baked cookies.

Softener for Dry Feet

2 tbsp. lanolin
1 tbsp. sweet almond oil
1 tbsp. glycerin
1 dropper oil of rose
1/2 dropper oil of patchouli

Warm lanolin over hot water, then add olive oil and glycerin. Add essential oils and store in glass jar.

This has a heady fragrance. It's heavy but worth the time it takes to rub it in.

Rose Clay Talcum

Clay
Rose essential oil

Work a few drops rose essential oil into clay powder. Sprinkle into your shoes to keep them smooth fitting and odor free.

Baking Soda or Salt Water Foot Bath

Soak feet in lukewarm water to which 1 tbsp. baking soda and a few drops of rose essential oil have been added.

Much of the dead skin can be rubbed off with a towel. You may need a pumice stone to get the rest off.

OR

Soak tired, swollen feet in warm salt water. Use about one cup salt to six inches bath water and add a few drops of rose essential oil for soothing fragrance.

Hair Affair

Your hair and how you wear it tells more about you than any other physical characteristic, and this has been true of both males and females in every known culture. Hair indicates age, social position, political attitudes and sex (sometimes). Changing your hairstyle is the quickest and easiest way to create a new appearance. Although hair, unlike skin, is dead, it requires as careful handling as a delicate fabric.

Over the centuries, except for the shaved heads of the women of ancient Egypt, who considered hair evil and wore wigs, long hair has been considered a beauty essential.

Depending on heredity and health, we'd have about 25 feet of hair on our heads by age 50 if it grew continually and never fell out or broke off. Average hair growth is one-third to two-fifths of an inch each month, accelerating a bit in warm weather. It grows fastest at night, and particularly between the ages of 15 to 25, noticeably slowing down beginning at age 30. At 50 there is another major decline in growth. It slows down to one-half its rate of growth when it reaches a length of about 10 inches. Normally, we shed between 50 and 100 hairs every day.

Ironically, a man holds the record for the longest hair of all time. According to Clairol Canada research he was an Indian monk, Swami Pandarasannadhi, whose hair grew 26 feet long.

Just as people have smeared all manner of things on their faces in the name of beauty, they have anointed their heads with all sorts of preparations including bear grease, beef marrow, skunk oil, fox grease, butter, and a mixture of honey and lye.

Saint Paul was so intrigued by women's hair that he ordered them to cover their heads in church so as not to tempt the devil—and possibly weak-willed saints.

Diane of Poitiers, a famous beauty (mistress of Henry II of France —20 years her junior), looked astonishingly young for her age. It is said she used only rain water for her hair as well as for her other ablutions. For those who would try a 'Poitier', rainwater may not be easy to come by. It can be replaced with distilled water, or borax powder (USP grade) can be added to water to soften it.

Homemade Rose Shampoo

1 cup powdered Castille soap
1/4 cup oil (olive, avocado or almond)
1/2 cup distilled water
Rose oil

Warm oil in double boiler then blend in soap. Add warmed distilled water and enough rose essential oil to suit your nose. Mix thoroughly. Use sparingly.

Use avocado or olive oil for dry hair, almond oil for oily hair.

Great Rinse

3 or 4 tbsp. red grape juice (unsweetened)
1 cup distilled water
Few drops rose essential oil

Mix ingredients and use as final rinse. It lightens and adds body to the hair.

Rose Hair Tonic

3 tbsp. alcohol (vodka)
1/8 tsp. rosemary oil
1/8 tsp. cinnamon oil
5 tbsp. rosewater

Dissolve the oils in the alcohol. Add the rosewater. Shake well.

A hair tonic, when massaged into the scalp and hair, stimulates the oils and blood in the scalp and may also be antiseptic.

Red Rose Vinegar Rinse

1 oz. dried rose petals (2 tbsp.)
1 pint white or cider vinegar

Cap and let stand for two weeks. Strain. Add 1 tbsp. to a gallon of water for final rinse.

Cider vinegar is great for brunettes, white vinegar great for blondes.

Flax Seed Hair Set

1 cup flax seed
3 cups rosewater

Simmer seeds in rosewater. Strain and thin to desired consistency. Flax seed is available in health food stores.

Rose Hot Oil Treatment

To prepare rose oil for the hot oil treatment, simmer one cup of dried rose petals in one pint of oil for 30 minutes. Strain. The rose oil should be used warm.

To give yourself the rose hot oil treatment, first shampoo your hair. Leave damp.

Section hair and pin up separated locks. Using cotton balls, pat warm rose oil all over scalp. Wrap head in hot towel for half an hour. When 30 minutes are up, remove towel and shampoo hair. A second shampoo will be necessary. You can use any oil for this treatment, although olive oil is a standard choice. Other excellent oils are peanut, safflower, walnut or wheatgerm. You may prefer safflower because it has little natural odor.

NOTE: Other herbs used with great success are: rosemary, lavender, sage, clove, comfrey and mullein.

Lip Balms & Rouges

Archaeologists have excavated lipsticks at the biblical city of Ur and it is known that the Egyptians and Romans used a liquid or paste including carmine to color their lips.

In oriental harems, veiled women dampened heady damask rose petals with sweet vanilla-spiked cream. They then forced the mixture through a piece of gauze to make seductive lip gloss. As this sweet pink salve did not keep well, it had to be made fresh each day.

In Victorian times, well-bred ladies made lip salves in their still-rooms but pawned off the rosy tint as natural.

Rouges are one of the oldest types of make-up and are mentioned in Roman writings. Rouges in the form of 'Spanish wool' and 'Spanish papers' were made in Spain from wool and paper, impregnated with red dyes from cochineal. They were dampened with water then rubbed on the cheeks and lips.

Rose Rouge

Petroleum jelly or talc
Beet juice or red food coloring
Rose oil

Spread a small amount of petroleum jelly (Vaseline) or talc in a saucer. Stir in a few drops of beet juice or food coloring and a few drops of rose essential oil. Mix until desired color is reached. If orange shade is desired, mix in a few drops of yellow food color.

Henna Cheeks

Touch up cheeks as the women in India do with a tiny bit of powdered henna. This gives a natural brownish tint. For a rose scent, grind two drops rose oil into the henna using a mortar and pestle.

Rose Lip Ice

1 tbsp. beeswax
1 tbsp. coconut oil
1 dropper rose oil

In small pan over hot water, melt beeswax and coconut oil. Remove from heat and add rose oil. While still warm pour into small container. This small amount goes a long way.

NOTE: You can use some rosemary oil, if desired. It has extraordinary healing properties.

Glycerine Lip & Cheek Gloss

1/2 cup cold cream
1/8 tsp. carmine
1 tsp. glycerine
Rose essential oil

Mix carmine with glycerine. Stir this mixture and several drops of rose essential oil into the cold cream.

Soaps

No one knows when soap was first discovered. Probably the oldest literary reference to soap is found in the 4000 year old clay tablets written by the Mesopotamians. One such recipe called for one part oil to five parts potash.

Pliny the Elder, the noted Roman scholar of the first century A.D., observed that soap was first used externally as a medicine, being of benefit in the disposal of scrofulous sores.

The first literary reference to soap as a means of cleansing a person or clothes is by the Greek physician Galen in the 2nd century A.D.

By the 13th century, soap had made its way to France and by the 14th century to England.

The French chemist, Eugene-Michel Chevreul, demystified soap in 1823 when he showed that saponification was a chemical process splitting fat and lye into soap (the alkali salt of fatty acids) and glycerine (which he named).

In one shop in London near Piccadilly, you can find white rose soap which contains genuine essence of roses. But why travel to London when you can make your own rose soap.

Making your own soap isn't any more difficult than making a cake. It does, however, seem like magic when you combine an evil-smelling, ugly-looking jar of lye with an equally unattractive batch of fat and come up with a beautiful bar of soap.

Simple Simon Soap

Bring one to two ounces water to just below the boiling point. Add pieces of pure white soap which will dissolve quickly (use leftovers of your choice). Add a few drops of rose oil and mix well. Pour into a container such as an egg poacher which has been greased with Vaseline. Allow to cool. The small circular cakes will smell of roses.

Simple Soap

2 tbsp. lye (rounded)
1/2 cup distilled water
1 cup lard (which must be melted and cooled or oil, ie. apricot, coconut)

OTHER INGREDIENTS YOU CAN ADD:

1 tsp. of honey to turn soap amber
Bran and oatmeal, with sandalwood and rose scent
Rose essential oil

In a GLASS container, measure the 1/2 cup cold distilled water. After donning rubber gloves, slowly add two tablespoons dry flaked lye, stirring constantly with a wooden spoon until the lye is dissolved. Because of a powerful chemical reaction, the water will quickly heat until it steams. These caustic fumes can 'catch' in the throat so prepare lye in a well-ventilated area, near an open window, and avert your face. Use extreme caution when handling lye.

Once both are cool (ie. the lye mixture and the lard) pour into each other, beating all the time with a wooden spoon (approx. 20 minutes).

Add other ingredients desired.

Grease molds with Vaseline (use plastic or wood—no metal when using lye) When almost ready to set, pour into molds. These could be heart-shaped ice-cube molds for guest soaps.

Cover the molds with plastic wrap or other cover (do not use aluminum foil). Take cover off in 24 to 30 hours.

Let set for 4 weeks (taste in 4 weeks—if it 'bites' it is still too strong). If it does not set, reheat mixture in microwave or in double boiler.

Easy Rose Soap Balls

If you don't want to start from scratch, you might enjoy preparing a fragrant rose soap made from any unscented soap such as Ivory.

1 bar unscented soap
1 tbsp. honey
1 tbsp. strong rosewater
1/2 tsp. rose oil
Finely ground rose petals, if desired

Grate one cup soap into enamel or porcelain pot. Add other ingredients. Place over hot water and melt, stirring frequently. When well blended remove from heat and beat in one tsp. rose oil. In dry hands, roll warm mixture into balls. Allow to dry for two days before use.

Rose-Lavender Soap Balls

Pour 1/4 cup boiling water over 1 tbsp dried pulverized mixture of lavender flowers and roses. Steep 15 minutes. Allow to cool.

Reheat till bubbly. Remove from heat and add 5 or 6 drops of rose (or lavender) oil, if a stronger scent is desired.

Pour over two cups shredded Ivory soap. Mix well with hands and let stand 15 minutes. Mix again and divide into three or six parts, rolling each into a ball. Place on plastic wrap and dry for three days. That's it!

Vegetarian Rose Soap

Strict vegetarians have limited options in cleaning products since most use at least some animal fats. The following soap is made entirely of vegetable oils. When well cured, this soap has a copious though some-what thin lather.

2 cups coconut oil or 100% solid vegetable shortening

3/4 cup cold soft water

1/4 cup lye flakes

Rose essential oil

Melt coconut oil until liquid but not too warm. It has a very low melting point, so don't overheat.

Add lye to cold water. Stir until dissolved.

Grease molds (no metal) generously with petroleum jelly.

When both mixtures are cool, pour lye into fat, stirring constantly. This recipe takes a long time to saponify—up to an hour. Stir occasionally as it thickens.

Pour into molds. Let harden for several weeks before using.

FOR FANCY SOAP MOLDS CATALOGUE contact:
Pourette Mfg. Co., P.O. Box 1520, Seattle, WA 98115

9

Medicine

Few plants have been used so much by druggists throughout the centuries as the rose. You wonder why the herbalists bothered to grow any other plant. Decoctions of red rose were used for headache, weak memory, wind, spots, scars, or pains in the eyes, throat, gums and ears. Powdered roses in wine cured women's ailments. You could choose an electuary of roses, sugar of roses, syrup of dried roses or honey of roses.

In Greece it was Hippocrates who separated medicine from philosophy and magical practices. He was knowledgeable in the preparation of herbs. A 'simple' is a medicinal herb or medicant obtained from a herb. Among the 400 simples used by Hippocrates was the rose.

The *Materia Medica* of Dioscorides (first century A.D.) contained as many as 600 plants. It is regarded as the earliest herbal in existence and was the source of herbal therapy for 16 centuries. In his herbal, cabbage, garlic, the lily, the mallow and the rose were all praised for their values.

In 900 A.D. Abu Ali Al-Husan Ibn Ahd Allah Ibn Sina—thankfully known as Avicenna—traveled extensively, writing many books on the properties of plants. He is credited with the invention of 'distillation', and used the rose as part of his first experiments. As a result, the Arabs became very famous for their perfumes and medicants.

During Norman times the rose was an essential part of the monastery garden, used not only for its medicinal properties but for flavoring meats. The part of the monastic garden devoted to roses was known as the roserie.

In the 13th century, King Thibaut IV of Navarre was away on a crusade in Arabia where he was struck by the perfume of a red rose. He was so attracted by it that when he returned home to France he brought it with him. It was grown at Provins where it was discovered that its perfume persisted no matter what was done with it. The apothecaries of the town took advantage of this; they powdered the dried petals and put them into pharmaceutical preparations. This developed into a substantial industry. The rose became known as the 'Apothecary's Rose' as well as the 'Provins Rose' *(R. gallica officinalis)*. Conserve of roses and infusion of roses are two of the medicinal preparations prepared from the petals of *R. gallica officinalis.*

Roses and Herbs in the Sick Room

Science has proved by analysis the medicinal value of many of the common herbs and flowers, including the rose.

Rose leaves, flowers and hips are therapeutically a mild astringent, aperient, diuretic; an aid to the liver, gall bladder, blood stream; a tonic/stimulant and a refrigerant (in the summer time).

An infusion of dried rose petals is taken for headache and dizziness and, with honey added, is a great nerve tonic and a 'blood purifier'.

A decoction of the petals serves to treat mouth sores; and a decoction made with wine invigorates the tired body and is useful in easing uterine cramps. The wine decoction also helps allay toothache, and used as a cold compress for the forehead, it relieves headache. As a warm trickle into the ear, it helps earache.

Cloths soaked with rose vinegar can also be used as a compress for headache; and rose honey is an ancient remedy for sore throat.

An old soother for headaches was a pillow filled with dried roses. A nap on the pillow is said to diminish a headache considerably.

Red Rose is Best

Red roses are considered best for medicinal use. Of the horticultural types, those classified as Hybrid Perpetuals are the most suitable. The following are the species most commonly used medicinally: *Rosa Californica, Rosa Centifolia, Rosa Damascena, Rosa Eglanteria, Rosa Gallica, Rosa Laevigata, Rosa Roxburghii.*

Tonic and Stimulant

Rose is a general tonic and fortifier, and has a particularly effective action on the nervous, circulatory and respiratory systems. It is good for all skin problems, from eczema, wrinkles and dryness to puffiness and congestion of the pores. For skin problems mix 2 to 3 drops in 2 teaspoons of almond oil.

The rose is also believed to be a sexual stimulant for women, and may help those who complain of frigidity. Make a body oil for special occasions by adding 3 to 6 drops of rose essential oil to 3 to 4 teaspoons of soya oil.

Rosewater

Rosewater is a simple and surprisingly effective eye-easer. Use it in compresses and for inflamed eyes.

Rosewater can be added to apple cider vinegar to make up cosmetic vinegar. Rosewater can also be used for eye washes and as a delicate yet non-allergic aroma for some ointments (to make Rosewater see COSMETIC section).

Healthy Rose Tea

The rose's malic and tartaric acids serve to rid gravel from the urinary tract. It is also reputed to be of value in 'dissolving out' gallstones. Try the following tea remedy.
1 cup hot water
1 tsp. dried ground rose leaves
2 or 3 crushed hips
Small amount chopped citrus rind
Pinch of peppermint, carnation, dictamnus and bee balm

Cover for 10 minutes. Stir, strain and sip the cupful three or four times a day. NOTE: For a simpler method add rose leaves and petals to Pekoe tea.

Tincture of Rose

This can be used as a hemorrhage or as a stomachic.
1 pint boiling water
1 oz. dried rose petals
15 drops of oil of vitriol
3 to 4 tsp. white sugar

Pour boiling water onto petals. Add oil of vitriol and sugar. Strain. Take 3 to 4 teaspoons—three or four times a day.

Salves and Lotions

Simple Rose Salve
8 oz. lard by weight
2 oz. or 4 tbsp. wax
Roses (other medicinal herbs if desired)

Simmer roses and herbs in lard. Strain. Melt wax, add lard mixture gradually and simmer for several hours with any other herbs desired. If preferred, the ingredients may be baked in the oven for several hours. Strain out the (sometimes burnt) plant material. Place in jar. The salve is ready when it hardens.

To make a stronger preparation, strain off the first batch of herbs and lard, add another handful of roses and herbs to the strained lard. Simmer again. Repeat as often as desired.

Healing Combinations
1. Roses, goldenseal and slippery elm: as an aid in healing and reducing infection, skin diseases such as ringworm, erysipelas, eczema and sores.
2. Roses and marigold leaves/flowers (*Calendula officinalis*): as an anti-septic to soothe chapped hands and varicose veins, reduce body scars and help control thread veins on the face, reduce inflammation, soothe sunburn and soften skin.
3. Roses and comfrey: to heal almost any kind of sore, bruise, abrasion, wound, rupture, hemorrhoid or ulcers. According to ancient herbal healers, this combination is effective for bones that either grind or fracture.

Oil Lotions
Steep any of the above herbal groups in any vegetable, nut or fruit oil. Use as medicated rubs. (see Simple Maceration Method in ESSENTIAL OIL section)

Petal Soother
To an insect bite, scratch or skin irritation, apply a wettened petal.

Spring Tonics
(see Herbal teas in DRINKS section)

Aromatherapy

From the earliest times essential oils of flowers, herbs, fruit, leaves and roots have been used for their healing, beautifying and soothing properties. At home one can benefit from these essences through bathing, inhalation and massage.

Aromatherapy is the treatment by essential oils, either internally or externally. Like yoga, it has its origins in the East, and, like yoga, its aim is to maintain and restore harmony of body and mind.

The therapeutic use of essential oils dates back to thousands of years before Christ where in India and China their healing powers were long recognized. They realized that the secrets of life were locked in flowers, seeds, roots, leaves or bark—either healing or harmful, depending on how they were used.

Montaigne, a 16th century French essayist, believed the medical world could advance the cause of health by the greater use of scents. He suggested that odors contain qualities to change ones attitudes and spirits, and according to the scent, can create differing effects in a person.

Gattefosse, a French chemist in the early 20th century, researched the medicinal qualities of herbal oils, quoting in articles examples of their benefits to the treatment of skin cancer, gangrene, burns and other ailments.

Rose Essential Oil Treatments

Essential oils have a life-enhancing quality unique to each plant. Rose essential oil is an antispasmodic, an astringent, a depurative (blood purative), a regulator of female sex organs, a laxative, a stimulant, an aphrodisiac, a sedative, an anti-depressant and a tonic for the heart, stomach, liver and uterus.

1. Other antispasmodic oils are: basil, bergamot, lavender, pennyroyal, rosemary and sandalwood.
2. Other astringents are: cedarwood, patchouli, rosemary and sandalwood
3. Another depurative is: eucalyptus

4. Another laxative is: camphor
5. Other stimulants are: cloves, peppermint, rosemary, lavender
6. Other skin tonics are: bergamot, rosemary

External Application
The penetrative power of essential oils is great enough for them to act on the organs sub-adjacent to the areas to which the topical applications are made. Use them in the following manner:

BATHS: approx. 4 to 10 drops
COMPRESSES: approx. 2 to 6 drops per 100 gms (30 gms = 1 oz.)
MASSAGE OILS: approx. 1 to 3 percent (10 to 30 drops per ounce)
INHALATION: 7 to 12 drops for every two pints water

An essential oil can be used alone, or you can use a mixture of three. The maximum treatment is six weeks for a daily dose and 24 weeks for a weekly dose.

Internal Application
Pure essential oils (not chemically produced) may be taken, diluted in sweetened water or on a lump of sugar.

WARNING: Some herbs should NEVER be taken internally such as cedar wood or leaves, camphor, wintergreen, cade (Juniper Tar), citronella, pine, rhodium, wormwood or any imitation or artificial oil.

Both methods, internal and external, are beneficial to the mind and body. The external application is possibly more beneficial because of the mysterious powers which the odiferous molecules of these oils have upon the brain via the olfactory nerves and the speed with which the oils can be absorbed through the skin and through the circulatory system.

Inhalation
Sprinkle a few drops of oil into a small bowl of boiling water. Hang head over bowl, put towel over head and breathe deeply. Inhalation is for the lungs and head. This is highly volatile with a profound effect on the emotional and mental level as well as the physical.

10

History, Emblems & Symbols

Historically Speaking

Fossil roses found in rock formations in Colorado and Oregon prove that wild roses date back 40 million years. They apparently originated in central Asia and spread all over the northern hemisphere, but inexplicably never crossed the equator. No truly wild roses have been discovered in the southern hemisphere.

The Chinese were probably the first to cultivate roses. Five hundred years before the birth of Christ, Confucius wrote of the roses in the Imperial Gardens.

The spread of the rose throughout Western Europe owes much to the advance of Islam. As the Arabs moved from Persia, which they conquered in the 7th century, the flowers of the Middle East, including the rose, followed them, eventually to Spain in the West (8th century on) and to India in the East (10th century). No doubt many roses were brought to Britain during the Roman invasion. They were also brought to Britain from the East during the Crusades (11th century on).

War of Roses Over the centuries the rose has been used frequently in coats of arms and more frequently still in badges. It served as a badge of battle as far back as the Trojan War. Homer wrote, "Roses adorned the shield of Achilles and the helm of Hector."

As the heraldic emblem of England—a rose under a crown—it can be seen in carvings and paintings; it has been a device on royal coats of arms and on coins since the time of Edward I who used a golden rose with a green stalk.

The use of the rose as a political emblem can be traced to the wars between the rival Houses of York and Lancaster.

The Red Rose of Lancaster and the White Rose of York were symbols of the terrible Wars of the Roses, a name given many years after they were fought to a series of dynastic civil wars in England, which occurred between 1455 and 1487. The name is derived from the white and red roses which were respectively the badges of the House of York and (after 1485) of the House of Lancaster.

The first battle of the Wars of the Roses took place at St. Albans in 1455 because York had become convinced that Queen Margaret and the chief minister, Edmund Beaufort, Duke of Sommerset, were scheming to destroy him.

Thirty bloody years later the wars ended when the two houses were united by the marriage of Henry Tudor to Elizabeth of York. The uniting of these two houses on the throne of England also united the red and white roses, establishing the Tudor Rose, whose red and white petals symbolize the two reconciled houses.

Mary Tudor took as her badge the Tudor rose and a pomegranate. Elizabeth I used the Tudor rose with her motto 'Rosa Sine Spina', the rose without a thorn.

Forms of Heraldic Rose The rose is represented in heraldry by a stylized form of the dog rose, being normally a flower of five petals though a cluster of five others may form an inner ring round the seeded centre. The tips of the sepals appear between the petals.

The tincture of the flower must be blazoned, since no one color is 'proper' to the rose.

In heraldry, the rose is a mark distinctive of the seventh son.

Rose of James In the 18th century Scottish and English royalists, fighting for the Stuart dynasty, drank a toast to 'The King Over the Water'— the exiled James II, who with his descendants, James Edward Stuart and his son Bonnie Prince Charlie, was living in France. Their Jacobite glasses were often engraved with a full-blown rose for James, and a bud for Prince Charlie.

White roses were linked with the Stuarts throughout history; Bonnie Prince Charlie wore a white rose in his hat as he marched to Derby.

Symbolism

Dr. Marie-Louise von Franz of Zurich, collaborator with Carl G. Jung, in Man and His Symbols, has explained the circle (or sphere) as a symbol of the Self. The abstract circle figures in Zen painting and abstract mandalas appear in European art. Some of the splendid examples are the rose windows of the cathedrals (see VISUAL ARTS section). These are representations of the Self of man transposed onto the cosmic plane.

A cosmic mandala in the shape of a shining white rose was revealed to Dante in a vision.

Emblems

Homer tells us that roses adorned the shield of Achilles while R. gallica was used as an emblem by the warriors of Persia some thousand years before the birth of Christ. This, the Persian rose, was described by Pliny the Elder as being brilliant red and is one of the oldest flowers still cultivated.

Enameled gold roses grace two of Great Britain's most prestigious decorations: the 600-year-old Order of the Garter and the Order of the Indian Empire.

Brazil's Order of the Rose, established by Emperor Pedro I in 1829, bears small enameled roses said to match the fair complexion of his wife, Princess Amelia.

Roses are used as emblems for many diverse organizations and occasions. The famous Kentucky Derby horse race is known as 'The Running of the Roses.'

A yellow rose is the emblem of the International Beta Sigma Phi Sorority, while the junior group, Nu Phi Mu, uses the pink rose in both song and ritual. The Order of the Rose is an honor awarded for loyalty to the organization.

Rose Bowl, Pasadena

Formally the Pasadena Tournament of Roses, this is the oldest American football contest held annually in Pasadena, California, on New Year's Day (or January 2nd if New Year's falls on a Sunday).

Each game is preceded by a Tournament of Roses parade or Rose parade and includes a Rose Queen and her princesses. The first festival, originally called The Battle of Flowers, was held on January 1, 1890. Local citizens decorated their carriages and buggies with flowers and drove over a prearranged route; the parade was followed by amateur athletic events. From 1897 on it was conducted by the Pasadena Tournament of Roses Association. Rose Bowl stadium opened in 1922.

Canada

The province of Alberta, Canada is *'Wild Rose Country'*. Roses are found wild only in the northern hemisphere and there are many natural varieties. The Alberta rose, the 'prickly rose', is a small shrub 3 to 4 feet high and spreads to form dense thickets. The subject of an official floral emblem for the province of Alberta was first raised in the Edmonton Journal in 1926. The Women's Institutes prompted the Department of Education to let the school children vote for their choice. The wild rose won and became Alberta's official flower in 1930.

USA

In 1986 President Ronald Reagan signed into law a measure designating the rose as the national floral emblem of the United States. The ceremony took place in the rose garden of the White House.

The search for a national flower had gone on since the 19th century with some 70 bills introduced promoting candidates ranging from the columbine to the mountain laurel. The debate had been enlivened by the perennial campaign of Senator Everett M. Dirksen on behalf of the 'robust, rugged, bright, stately' marigold.

The rose is the emblem of some U.S. states:
   Georgia: the state flower is 'Cherokee'; white, gardenia-like
      Chinese rose and very fragrant (1916)
   Iowa: the state flower is 'Wild Rose' (1897)
   North Dakota: the 'Wild Rose'
   New York State: the Rose (1955)
   District of Columbia: American Beauty Rose

Britain

The national emblem of England is the Tudor rose, 'Rosa alba', the result of a cross between the Damask rose and England's native rose, 'R. canina', a white rose charged upon a red rose. R. alba bears its flat ivory-white flowers early in summer and possesses the powerful scent of the Damask rose. The uniting of the Houses of Lancaster and York after the Wars of the Roses resulted in the combining of the two emblems.

"Buy my lovely roses" was the cry of flower-sellers of the streets of London, and it has been suggested that the island was named Albion after Rosa alba, the scented white rose.

United Kingdom

The badge of the United Kingdom includes the rose, thistle and shamrock engrafted on the same stem.

Iran

The rose is the national flower of Iran.

Syria

The country of Syria took its name from the word Suri, which means 'land of roses'. So profusely did the pink Damask rose bloom around that area of Syria bordering Lebanon that it gave its name to the town of Damascus.

Currency

Many nations have used the rose on their currency. In ancient Rhodes (after rhodon, the Greek word for rose), the rose was adopted as that island's traditional floral symbol and was stamped on 102 of their coins over a period of several centuries. These coins were widely circulated and used as currency throughout the Mediterranean.

It has appeared on English coins since 1344 when Edward III used its outline on a gold coin, later known as the 'noble.' The rose is also shown on the two shilling-piece of Queen Elizabeth II.

By 1722 the rose had found its way into the currency of the United States, embellishing the Rosa Americana coin with a stylized Tudor rose, a five petaled bloom; in 1856 a Kansas territorial bank issued a three dollar bill festooned with a trio of rose-laden cupids.

Stamps

Stamps picturing flowers are one of the most popular categories in topical collecting with more than 3000 stamp designs featuring flowers or plants. Switzerland was the first country to bring the beauty of a flower to a postage stamp and the first to realize the publicity value of picturing native flowers in full color on stamps.

On stamps the rose often had symbolic meaning. It was used to commemorate the rescue of a 1938 Russian polar expedition, the 350th anniversary of the birth of the Peruvian saint, St. Rosa of Lima (1586–1617), and the first anniversary of the death of the Indian leader, Jawaharal Neru.

Roses and orchids are the two most popular flower stamps. One edition of three rose stamps was issued by New Zealand for the 1971 World Rose Convention.

In Austria, the rose is symbolic of Christmas—an Austrian rose stamp of 1937 was the first stamp specifically intended for holiday greetings.

In North America libraries carry the Scott Standard Postage Catalogue which contains the stamps of the world.

Canada

In the 1964-66 series of provincial flowers and coats of arms, the Alberta 'Wild Rose' was depicted on the 5 cent stamp.

A 1981 Canadian 17 cent stamp features the 'Montreal Rose'.

USA

Catalogue #1876	1981	'Rose'
1953-2002	1982	State birds and flowers
2014	1982	'International Peace Garden'

United Nations

266	1975	'Wild Rose Growing from Barbed Wire'

Great Britain

786-789	1976	'Elizabeth of Glamis', 'Grandpa Dickson', 'Rosa Mundi' and 'Sweet Briar'

Monaco

1311	1981	'Catherine Deneuve Rose' issued for the first International Rose Competition in Monte Carlo, June 1982

Switzerland

B152	1945	'Alpine Dog-Rose'
B252	1956	'Women's Work', a rose, a spoon and a pair of scissors

Italy

1452	1981	'Roses'

Mali

C55	1968	'Roses and Anemones' by Van Gogh

11

Ritual, Mysticism & Spells

The Persians and their wise men, the Magi, who were venerated far and wide for their knowledge, held the rose in high esteem. Red like the color of fire, it attracted the fire worshippers of the 12th century B.C. who cultivated it for their religious ceremonies and placed it under the special protection of an archangel.

The Christians created a whole new line of legends. The wild briar rose with its five petals was associated with the five wounds of Christ—a symbol of His blood.

With the decline of the Roman Empire the early Christian church rejected the rose. It reminded the church too much of the Romans who had found entertainment in watching Christians devoured by lions. To the Christians it was a symbol of decadence. Cultivation practically ceased, except in a few monastery gardens, until the time of Charlemagne. Even after that, roses were mainly used as a medicine.

But the rose, associated with Venus, was far too beautiful to remain banished, and in the 1200's roses once more became widespread and appreciated. In an about-switch, it soon became one of the symbols of the Virgin Mary, the 'Rose of Heaven'. The white rose became the symbol for the Immaculate Conception. Her roses were thornless because she herself was said to be without thorns, free from original sin.

In the Middle Ages there was a festival called Rose Sunday, which perpetuated the belief that after her ascent to heaven the Virgin's tomb was found filled with roses and lilies.

In Velasquez's painting of 'The Coronation of the Virgin', God is placing upon her head a garland of red and white roses.

There is a very old belief that all roses were originally white and turned red only after blood had been spilt on them. Many popes began to use the rose as their seal or crest.

Roses, especially red roses, almost inevitably stem from spilt blood —blood from the foot of Venus pursuing Adonis, from the dead Adonis himself, or on a more sombre level from the blood of Christ (the Crown of Thorns was made of rose briars).

The Islamic belief is more earthy; roses are supposed to spring from sweat dripping from Mohammed's brow. The Hindus have tales involving Vishnu and Brahma, and Lakshmi, who was born from a rose and became Vishnu's consort.

Saint Rose of Lima (1586-1617)

Saint Rose of Lima was the first person born in America to be canonized by the Roman Catholic Church. She took the name Rosa de Santa Maria and wore a crown of rose thorns under her habit. In 1667 Pope Clement X proclaimed her patron saint of South America. On her feast day, August 30, roses decorate the church in her memory.

The Rosary

The word rosary comes from the Latin 'rosarium' meaning rose garden. Prayers are recited and counted on a string of beads or knotted cord. The use of the rosary, as part of a religious exercise, is widespread occurring in Buddhism, Christianity, Hinduism and Islam. The most common rosary is the rosary of the Blessed Virgin Mary.

In Hinduism the rosary differs according to the sect using it. The Buddhist rosary usually contains 108 beads. Its use undoubtedly originated in India. In Tibet, the rosary was used by both monks and laity for prayer and divination. Made of varying materials, its color related to the divinity worshipped.

The rosary used by Moslems usually has 99 beads relating to the 99 names of Allah. Jewish rosaries have no religious use. Rather, they serve to occupy the hands on Sabbaths and holy days when work is forbidden.

Whatever the date Christians began this practice in Europe, the devotional use of beads had been established long before in the East. The Sanscrit term japa-mala, 'muttering chaplet', describes the rosary as a means of recording the number of prayers muttered.

In the Roman Catholic church, a rosary consists of 15 decades, designed to assist a scheme of prayer and meditation. Each decade contains 10 Ave Marias, marked by small beads, preceded by a pater noster, marked by a larger bead, and concluded by a Gloria Patri. Five decades make a chaplet, which is a third part of the rosary. The beads help to guide the course of devotion and to record its progress.

The Roman Catholic Church celebrates a Feast of the Rosary on October 7 which is also the anniversary of the Christian victory over the Turks at Lepanto in 1571. The liturgical recitation of the rosary is believed to have contributed to this victory.

Dante's Divine Comedy

In the Paradiso section of Dante Alighiere's 'The Divine Comedy', the rose appears in Paradiso—where Beatrice presents it to Dante on arriving in the Garden of Paradise, which is itself constructed as a rose. Here, the rose symbolizes perfection, consummate achievement, and ultimately the great mystery of the Trinity and the union of God with man.

The Golden Rose

The Golden Rose is an ornament of wrought gold, blessed by the Pope on the fourth Sunday in Lent. It is said to have originated in 1050 with Leo IX and it became a custom of the Pope to send it as a mark of favor to a foreign sovereign, a notable Roman Catholic personage, a city, or a church congregation.

In the early years of his reign, Henry VIII twice received the golden rose. Among other recipients were Napoleon III and Isabella II of Spain.

On the first Sunday in Lent, the Pope bestows a cluster of roses of purest gold on Our Lady, after giving it his blessing.

Over the centuries, the golden rose has gradually become more ostentatious with jewelled ornamentation.

Sub Rosa

The Romans believed that Cupid dedicated the rose to Harpocrates, God of Silence, as a bribe to be quiet about his mother's indiscretions. Ever since, secrecy has been connected with roses. It was an appropriate dedication, the petals covering the stamens the way our lips cover our mouths.

At banquets fresh roses were hung from the ceilings to encourage guests to show the same discretion as Harpocrates; nothing should be repeated that was said 'under the rose' or sub rosa.

Centuries later, plasterwork roses served the same purpose, and one of the loveliest examples is carved on the colonnades of the Piazza Della Signoria in Florence.

The church adopted the pagan Roman use of 'sub rosa' meaning secretly, privately, or in a manner that forbids disclosure. Roses were placed on the tops of confessionals to guarantee privacy. Pope Hadrian gave permission for roses carved from wood to take the place of these fresh flowers.

Baillee des Roses

The 'Baillee des Roses' existed in France until the end of the 16th century. It consisted of a tribute of roses which were given by the peers of France to the Parliament. Each peer, in turn, had to see that the rooms of the palace were strewed with roses, other flowers and sweet herbs. As the peer went through the rooms, he carried a large silver bowl containing crowns of roses for every member of the Parlement.

Memorial Rose

'Wichuraiana' or memorial rose is a creeping plant or almost that. It was sold by nurserymen years ago for use in planting on graves in cemeteries. It is reasonably hardy, holds its foliage most of the winter. The flowers are single white. Since the white rose is a symbol of virginity, a rose of this color was often planted on the grave of a virgin.

Roses have long been associated with death. From Roman times flowers were often thrown on graves, and Roman wills sometimes specified that roses be planted on the graves. A Greek and Roman custom was the planting of rose bushes on May 11, the day commemorating the dead, known as *'Dies Rosae'*.

The Syrians used the rose as an emblem of immortality as did the Chinese and Greeks who carved it on their tombs.

In parts of Switzerland, cemeteries are still known as 'rose gardens'. In Turkey, flowers are sometimes carved on tombstones of women.

John Aubrey, the diarist, records the planting of red roses on the graves of sweethearts. The surviving partner, who was not supposed to re-marry, looked after the roses and regularly re-turfed the grave.

The Saxons believed that when a child died the figure of death could be seen leaving the house to pick a rose outside.

Everything's Coming Up Roses

Roses do well in cemeteries. With good reason.

A human body of average size contains almost two kilos of nitrogen, together with worthwhile quantities of calcium and other nutrients. Dried blood and bone meal, after all, are the classic fertilizer of the rose grower and gardener. Like any organic tissue, a body decays to form humus which improves the moisture holding capacity of soils without creating water-logging and is, in all other respects, a horticultural 'good thing'.

According to an article by David Welch in the May 1988 issue of The Rose (magazine of the The Royal National Rose Society), the "regular rows of graves in modern British cemeteries permit the use of roses in long formal beds, where they reduce the cost of maintenance because grass is an expensive material to care for in and amongst the headstones".

He describes one particular cemetery near the middle of Aberdeen, Scotland, called Nellfield where the graves had sunk so much that it was pitted and dangerous to walk there. The headstones had tilted and were insecure. The undergrowth was shoulder high. He says it was an affront to citizens.

Nellfield cemetery is now one of the better rose gardens in the country, containing 74 varieties, mainly of Cluster Flowered hybrids. "There are 78,000 bushes in an area of 6 acres. It is enclosed by high granite walls, in places 10 feet high, and it is near the heart of a major city," says Welch.

You can still find many old roses thriving in cemeteries and in old or abandoned farmsteads. Most of these old roses grow easily from cuttings, so you can add these nameless survivors to your garden.

Rosicrucians The rose cross, a combination of a rose and a cross, is the symbol of the Rosicrucians, an order of philosophers. The Rosicrucians have been known by various names, such as Brothers of the Rosy Cross, Rosy-Cross Knights, and Rosy-Cross philosophers.

To the Rosicrucians the rose represents evolution, while the cross represents the labors and burdens of life and the karma which we must endure in our earthly existence.

The fraternity still exists, and is a non-religious secret society of metaphysicians and philosophers. The fraternity devotes itself to the study of the secrets of nature.

Magic In many traditions of magic, the rose symbolizes self-fulfillment and the blossoming of the personality.

Aromatics in The Church In Egypt, herbal essences were in common use both as medicinal aids and as body beautifiers. Among those who used aromatics were the Egyptian priests. Not only were aromatics used for therapeutic and cosmetic purposes, but they also served a vital purpose in religious ceremony.

A fragrant plant or flower was connected with all the ancient mysteries—the myrtle of Venus, the verbena of the Druids, the mystical lotus of India, and the rose of Isis.

In the Middle Ages, the monasteries each had their own private herbaria and herbal books for reference. The old and the sick were often taken into their care and given herbal potions and concoctions. Roses were prominent in many of these remedies and some of the great monastery rose gardens, then established, still exist today.

Do It Yourself with Roses

1. MAKE A ROSARY: From rose beads (see recipe in WEARING section). These rose beads can also be strung with icons or beads of glass. The Rosary was so named because the first beads were made from roses.

   In the Mediterranean countries, rose petals were crushed into a mortar-like paste, then partially dried. This process of moistening and drying was repeated until the paste became so hard that it was possible to cut off tiny fragments which were shaped and polished like beads. A small hole was made in them so they could be strung on twine and kept indefinitely. (A contemporary told the authors that his great grandmother's rosary was made from roses and still retains its scent.)

2. MAKE ROSE INCENSE: Using the following recipe to add a touch of mystery or sanctity to your home.
   (see method in PERFUMING THE HOUSE section).

Frankincense, Myrrh & Rose Incense
4 tbsp. sawdust
1 tsp. cinnamon powder
1 tsp. clove powder
2 tsp. dried fragrant rose petals powdered
2 tbsp. frankincense
2 tbsp. myrrh
OR experiment with your own mixture.

3. RUB WOODEN CANDLESTICKS or wooden table altar with rose oil.
   Use rose candles.

4. HANG ROSES from the ceiling or lamps for 'sub rosa'.

Pocket Full of Passion—Love Charm Let your imagination take
wing. Carry on with a love spell.

One of the best days for operations dealing with love is Friday.
Friday is ruled by Venus who rules roses. The best time is evening or night
when there are fewer distractions, when you feel more 'enclosed', and
when the subconscious is readying itself for the deep world of dreams.

The spell-maker should be alone. To add more atmosphere, burn
rose candles in a 3 or 7 branched candlestick, which allude specifically to
magic. When the spell is finished, pinch out (never blow out) the flame.
As you light the candles, you recite your chosen words to strengthen the
bond of sympathetic magic. You might start with something along the
lines of:

> *As this candlestick burns, so may (NAME) burn with*
> *love for me.*
> *As this wax melts, so may (NAME) heart melt with*
> *love for me.*

Your incantation should cause desire to wax full in your lover's
soul.

Most important, to incite the passions of your beloved, the essential
ingredients are attitude, atmosphere and the power of suggestion. Keep
your mind firmly upon the purpose of the spell. When we cast a spell we

are using the power of our 'deep mind' to send messages to the 'deep mind' of another.

> *"The base of all forms of magic, however or by whomever used, must be the same fundamentally, and that base is Mind. Mind is the instrument, the channel, and perhaps in some cases the creator, of the forces which produce 'magical results'"* .
>
> JUSTINE GLASS

Unrequited Love Ritual A spine-tingling ritual from ancient days could make a girl haunt her erring lover in dreams until in desperation he returned to her. For this ritual three roses must be picked on Midsummer Eve. One is to be buried under a yew tree, the second in a newly dug grave. The third must be put under a girl's pillow for three nights and then burned.

Anyone who survives this ritual deserves to get her lover back.

12

Love & Marriage

A White Rose

The red rose whispers of passion
And the white rose breathes of love;
O, the red rose is a falcon,
And the white rose is a dove.

JOHN BOYLE O'REILLY

Symbol of Love From the days of Solomon, the rose has persisted as a symbol of love. It was sacred to both Venus, the goddess of love, and Bacchus, god of wine. Portraits of the goddess often show her crowned with roses or carrying a rose scepter, while on certain occasions a statue of Bacchus would be crowned with a rose.

A classical legend says that when Venus ran through a rose hedge to meet the wounded Adonis, her blood stained the flowers for all eternity.

Another story says that Eve gave us the red rose—that when she kissed the white rose in the Garden of Eden it blushed deep pink with pleasure.

The rose is also connected with Cupid who is typically shown with bow, arrow and roses.

Read in these Roses the sad story
Of my hard fate, and your own glory;
In the white you may discover
The paleness of a fainting lover;

In the red the flames still feeding
On my heart with fresh wounds bleeding.
The white will tell you how to languish,
And the red express my anguish. . . .
                                        CAREW

Sacred Language   At different times and places, people have used
flowers to form a sacred language, each flower having a special meaning.
Some flower codes were religious, some legal, some spoke of love as the
one Charles the II of Sweden brought back from the Ottoman Empire in
1714.

   To 'say it with flowers' soon spread through the courts of Europe.
Meanings varied, but basically the red rose said: 'I love you passionately'.

Don Juans   Roses are the Don Juans of the herbal world. They have
lovers everywhere. Take the British for example; there are ten times more
roses on the island than people.

   Yet even the Brits love affair with the rose pales beside that of the
Romans. Theirs was an Antony and Cleopatra love affair—an affair yet
to be rivalled. The Romans walked on roses, talked on roses, slept on roses
and made love on roses. They ate them, they drank them and made pillows
of them. Rosewater gushed from their fountains—they bathed in it, used
it as a skin lotion, sprinkled it on their beds and floors.

Perfume of Love   Both rose and musk with their
heady odors have been associated with love-
making for centuries. The ancient Greeks
considered perfume to be a gift of the
gods. No self-respecting Athenian would
receive a lover without first being properly perfumed.

   Some of the more fashionable among
the Classical elite would apply a different
scent to each part of their body.

   Because rose perfume is an exciter of love, it is best that you and this
scent are never too far apart. Its perfume assures you that even on the
hottest and sweatiest of days your odor will be lovely.

An Aphrodisiac   Certain essential oils, among them rose oil, are praised for their aphrodisiac properties. One of the reasons they work so fast is because they act directly on the limbic portion of the brain, which is also responsible for modulating sexual behavior.

Roses were used in very early times in lovephilters.

Valentine's Day   On Valentine's Day the rose, usually pink or red, holds a place of honor at Cupid's side. The color red is the symbol of warmth and feeling—the color of the human heart. A single red rose sent to a lover (or received from a secret admirer) is a message of love.

Green leaves stand for hope in a love affair. A custom passed down by British girls that you might want to try is to place bay leaves sprinkled with rosewater on your pillow on St. Valentine's Day eve. The girls hoped to see in their dreams the faces of their future husbands:

> *Good Valentine, be kind to me;*
> *In dreams, let me my true love see.*

An Old English wives tale says if you fold a rose in half and it splits your love is returned. If it does not split you are out of luck.

If a young girl had several lovers, and wished to know which would be her husband, she would take a rose leaf for each of her sweethearts, and naming each leaf after one of her lovers, she would watch them until one after another they sank, and the last to sink would be her future husband.

Valentine Cards   A rose on a Valentine card stands for love, a meaning that stretches back to classical mythology when the rose was the flower of Isis, Aphrodite and Venus. In the 'Romance of the Rose', written around 1200, the rose is described as being situated in the mysterious tabernacle of the garden of love of the chevalrie (knighthood) to which all men should aspire.

The roses on early Valentines were usually drawn or painted by hand. Some were made of pressed petals or flowers with painted stems and leaves.

The earliest Valentines were folded, sealed with wax, and delivered in person or left in some location where the recipient would surely find them. Many were sent anonymously, without signature or place of origin.

Many love-struck creators turned to cryptograms, puzzles, rebuses, acrostics and other devices to cloak their messages and identity from prying glances by anyone but their true loves.

By the middle of the 19th century the symbols that were to become standard were evolving—bunches of roses, red hearts, Cupid with his bow and arrows, etc.

Mistresses In ancient Greece lovers festooned the doorways of their mistresses homes with garlands of roses and other flowers.

Do It Yourself with Roses

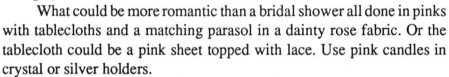

Recipe for A Rose Bridal Shower

What could be more romantic than a bridal shower all done in pinks with tablecloths and a matching parasol in a dainty rose fabric. Or the tablecloth could be a pink sheet topped with lace. Use pink candles in crystal or silver holders.

Centre the table with a bouquet of roses surrounded by bowls of beautiful tussie mussies and beribboned baskets of rose sachets.

Make tussie mussies (nosegays) of baby's breath centred with pink roses and lavender. Grace the bouquets with long pink streamers tied with love knots.

Give the guests heart-shaped sachets as well as rose placecards or give them the tussie mussies as party favors.

Design your shower invitations with pressed rose petals, and have the guests sign on a rose scroll. Present the bride to be and both mothers with rosebud corsages.

For refreshments make rose sandwiches and place on a tray lined with parsley, lettuce and radish roses. Serve with Raspberry Rose Punch garnished with fresh mint and rose petals. Surround the punch bowl with a living rose wreath.

For dessert serve the Genoese Rose Cream (see FOOD section for recipes).

Ask the guests to bring roses (which they have dried) from their gardens to make into a potpourri for the bride (see section on POTPOURRI).

Give a short talk on roses and love.

Cut the rose pictures from a garden catalogue and post in the room. Give each guest a list of names to match to the appropriate rose picture.

Give small 'rose' prizes: rose notepaper, a tiny bottle of rosewater or perfume, rose sachets, or rose petal filled potholders.

Tussie Mussie
(NOSEGAY)

The Elizabethans carried little nosegays of fresh herbs and flowers called tussie mussies to overpower objectionable odors. A tussie mussie is a tightly gathered bouquet of herbs and flowers that expresses a personal message through the language of flowers.

Some herbs that you might include with roses in the nosegay are: basil (love, good wishes), burnet (a merry heart), marjoram (joy, happiness), rosemary (remembrance).

Today these little herbal bouquets are sometimes carried by brides.

TO MAKE A TUSSIE MUSSIE: Start with a circle or border of scented leaves. Add sprigs of herbs to fill the centre and accent with roses. Secure the bouquet with a rubber band and trim the stems to three of four inches.

Cut an 'X' in two paper doilies or lace circles and slip the stems through. Cover stems with florists tape if desired. Cut two 18 inch lengths of narrow ribbon. Tie both of these in a bow at the base with love knots added at the four ends. Tie a card to a streamer explaining the meanings of the herbs and flowers.

Make the tussie mussie from fresh materials and let dry naturally in a warm dry place. Or start with dried sprigs of herbs and roses and wire it all together. Sprinkle with a bit of orris root or other fixative and add a few drops of rose oil.

Another way to dry the nosegays is to put the entire tussie mussie in silica or sand, completely covering the bouquet.

Leave for two weeks (see section on DRIED ARRANGEMENTS in TABLE AND DINING ROOM DECOR).

Rose Corsage

Fresh roses
Leaves (your choice)
Fine wire
Floral tape
Ribbon

Put roses in water several hours so that it soaks up into the flower head through the stem. Cut off stem just below blossom. Cut piece of wire approximately 8 inches long and put through the calyx (the green part where flower and stem join) leaving four inches wire each side. Bring ends of wire together and twist to make stem. Wire the leaves by making a little stitch through the base.

When you have wired several flowers and leaves, arrange them in the design you want and twist the wire stems together into one main stem. Wind with florists tape so wire does not show. Fold ribbon into several loops and wind wire tightly around middle to make a bow. Leave long enough ends on the wire to fasten the bow to main stem of corsage.

Rose Table Napkin

Use a three inch napkin holder or glass. Fold the napkin in half, keeping the folded edge on top. Starting at one end, begin to roll it tight until you have a solid centre core, using about two inches of fabric.

Holding the centre tightly, gradually wrap the remainder of the fabric loosely around the centre, pinching it with your fingers as you go.

When you have completed this, fold in half the extra fabric that is hanging down. Tuck the fold into the glass or tall napkin ring. Work with it and shape it into .... A Rose!

Rose Placecards

These can be used for showers or dinner parties.

Stiff rose colored paper

Rose stickers

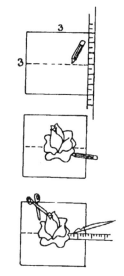

Cut paper into three inch squares. Draw a dotted line across the centre. In centre of card, place a rose sticker with the stem and part of the rose below the centre line and the remaining rose above it, but the rose should stop at least 1/4 of an inch from the top edge of the card as shown.

Score lightly along centre line 'from the outside edge up to the beginning of the rose on each side'. Do not score across rose.

TO SCORE: Hold ruler against dotted line. Run an exacto knife or small paring knife along rulers edge very lightly, cutting only surface of paper. Do not cut through paper.

With knife or scissors, cut around top of rose above centre line. Fold top half of each card down and back, leaving rose sticking up. Write guest's name under rose.

Using Roses at Weddings

"Marriage is like life in this — that it is a field of battle, and not a bed of roses".   R.L. STEVENSON

Ancient wedding customs featuring roses were revived during the Elizabethan age; many of today's ceremonial traditions are based on Elizabethan custom.

The Elizabethan family played a big part in the celebration. Before the bride awoke, the servants and family were busy preparing the house. They were up all night dusting, scrubbing, cooking. Rosemary and roses were placed in all the rooms and corridors, forming a soft carpet of blossoms. In ancient Rome, hundreds of roses were twined with myrtle into bridal garlands.

Meanwhile down at the groom's house, his men were busy adorning him with rosettes and ribbon streamers in colors chosen by the bride.

Roses are among the traditional flowers for a bridal bouquet; there is a white grandiflora named 'June Bride.' In the west of Scotland if a white rose bloomed in autumn it was a token of an early marriage.

As far as coordinating roses with the bride's dress, these days anything goes, but white roses are used the most. For the groom and his attendants, single roses make elegant and inexpensive boutonnieres.

The flower girl can go down the aisle dropping rose petals from a white wicker basket. During nuptial ceremonies in ancient Greece, roses were strewn along the path of the newlyweds as a sign of their friends good wishes.

Fragrant rose petal potpourri or rose petals can be thrown at weddings instead of rice (see PERFUMING THE HOUSE section).

Or, throw scented pink wedding rice made of rice, rosemary and rosebuds.

To end the ceremony or at the reception, the bride and groom can present a single long-stemmed rose to their mothers-in-law.

For further hints for a rose wedding reception, see FOOD section.

13

Literature & Legends

It was roses, roses
all the way
ROBERT BROWNING

The rose has a literature of its own. More legends and traditions centre around it than any other flower. The Ancient Greeks, when they wished to pay graceful compliments to their orators, would say "they spoke roses."

The ancient city of Rhodes was named after the Greek word 'rhodon' which means 'rose.'

Rose Poetry Throughout history poets have extolled the rose. The love of roses had strengthened in Persia from age to age; the roses of Shiraz were famous, and the rosewater from them was sent far afield.

In the 11th and 12th centuries the great Persian philosopher and poet Omar Khayamm expressed the love of his nation for roses in his Rubaiyat. There are at least eight references to the rose in it. Familiar to many are the lines: "Each Morn a thousand Roses...." and, "I sometimes think that never blows so red/the roses where some buried Caesar bled;" so too "the sigh of regret that Spring should vanish with the rose."

A damask rose was planted over Omar's grave at Naishapur. A seedling from it was planted in 1893 on the grave of Edward Fitzgerald at Boulge in Suffolk. Fitzgerald translated Omar's Rubaiyat into English. From this seedling many plants have been established elsewhere.

"Let us crown ourselves with rose-buds," says the Book of Wisdom and during Medieval times, garlands of roses were the symbol of heavenly joy. Chaucer, in his tales told to the Canterbury pilgrims on their way to the shrine of St. Thomas a Becket, wrote:

> *Thou with thy gerland wrough of rose and lilie,*
> *Thee, mene I, maid and martir, St. Cecilie.*

Among other famous rose poems are these by Burns and Shakespeare:

> *O, my Luve's like a red red rose*
> *That's newly sprung in June:*
> *O my Luve's like the melodie*
> *That's sweetly play'd in tune.*
>> ROBERT BURNS

> *What's in a name? that which we call a rose*
> *By any other name would smell as sweet.*
>> WILLIAM SHAKESPEARE
>> 'Romeo and Juliet'

> *A color like the red rose on triumphant brier.*
>> 'A Midsummer Night's Dream'

The famed German poet, Rainer Maria Rilke, sees the whole meaning of the universe in a bowl of roses. In an extravagant outpouring of nine verses comprised of 72 lines, he marvels:

> *"So much! So strangely tender. Where do we know of anything like this? Now before you stand the bowl of roses, The unforgettable, Giving beyond all power of giving...The world and wind and rain and patience of the springtime. And even the melting, fleeing, forming of the clouds and the vague influence of distant stars. . . now lies heedless in those open roses."*

Rose Theatre Shakespeare's 'Titus Androndicus' had its first performance in the Rose Theatre which was built on an old rose garden .The theatre was torn down in 1605. In just 16 years it played its part in a great flowering of English literature under playwrights such as Shakespeare and Christopher Marlowe. Its rival was the famous Globe Theatre, built a stone's throw away in 1599. Competition from the Globe and other Bankside theatres forced the Rose to close in 1603.

In 1989 archaeologists began excavating the site where this irregular 14-sided theatre stood. They uncovered a small, shallow stage (20 feet deep and up to 43 feet wide) as well as the bases of chalk and brick walls that supported seating under a thatched roof, for which spectators would have paid an extra penny or two.

The Rose, the only English Tudor theatre whose remains have been discovered, was built in 1587. It was the fourth Elizabethan theater in London and the first on Banckesyde (Bankside), an infamous area of brothels, inns, gaming houses and bear-baiting rings on the south side of the Thames.

Developers are planning to construct an office tower on the site of the theatre. The Heritage Preservation Society with the help of many actors, including Vanessa Redgrave, are attempting to preserve the old theatre by giving readings at the site and picketing the work crews.

In June of 1989 the construction crews filled the site with sand which was then covered with concrete to protect it while the construction is underway. The office tower will be built on stilts with the intention of later uncovering the theatre to make the heritage site available to the public.

Roses Speak Their Own Language Symbolically speaking the rose designates perfection, elegance, romance and love. The Greek poetess Sappho in her 'Ode to the Rose' called it "the Queen of Flowers".

The interpretations of the meanings of roses are as varied as the sources researched. Some of the most commonly recognized are:

ROSE, FULL-BLOWN
    I love you
ROSE, PINK
    Our love is perfect happiness
ROSE, WITHERED
    Reproach and fleeting beauty
ROSE, RED
    Love and desire
    Dedicated to Aphrodite and Venus
    Flower of Eros and Cupid
ROSE, WHITE
    Charm and innocence
    Emblem of Harpocrates (Greek)

Symbol of secrecy and silence
Flower of the Virgin Mary
ROSE, YELLOW
Infidelity and jealousy
Bad luck gift to a woman
ROSEBUD
Beauty and youth
ROSE OF JERICHO
Symbol of resurrection

Rosary While most of us think of the rosary as a string of beads, there are other meanings:

1. A bed of roses or a rose garden.
2. A garland of flowers.
3. A collection of beautiful quotations, especially poetical extracts.
4. A counterfeit coin of the reign of Edward I, worth about a halfpenny, coined abroad and brought surreptitiously into England. It was called a rosary because it bore the figure of a rose.
5. In zoology, a rope of eggs laid by the obstetrical frog or toad, and wound about the body in the shape of a rosary.

Mythology

Many stories surround the rose including the following tales. Tell them to your children and start your own tradition of rose fairy tales.

Beauty & The Beast In Beauty and the Beast, the famous fairy tale by Madame de Villeneuve, the young heroine asks her father for the gift of a rose rather than gowns or jewels. When the father attempts to fulfill Beauty's request by picking a rose in the Beast's garden, the Beast condemns him to death.

Read the outcome of this wonderful story from any good book of old fairy tales.

Alice Another rose tale is in 'Alice in Wonderland' by Lewis Carroll. Three gardeners paint a white rose tree red. When Alice asks why they are painting the roses red, they reply, "Why, the fact is, you see, miss, this here ought to have been a red rose tree and we put a white one in by mistake, and if the Queen was to find out we would all have our heads cut off, you know. . . ."

In the chapter, Garden of Live Flowers, in 'Through the Looking Glass', a talking rose tells Alice "You're beginning to fade, you know—and then one can't help one's petals getting a little untidy!"

The Nightingale & The Rose   In a poetic but sadder tale, 'The Nightingale and the Rose,' based on an ancient Persian legend, Oscar Wilde tells of a student's distress that he cannot find a red rose which his sweetheart has demanded. A nightingale gives up its life, singing all night long with the thorn piercing its heart so that the bush may produce a red rose. Alas, the girl refuses the rose saying that it will not go with her dress and besides someone has sent her jewels that "cost far more than flowers."

Legends of The Middle Ages

The Laurin Rose Garden   To the Scandinavian, the rose was under the protection of fairies and dwarfs and their king Laurin.

In olden days, so legends say, Laurin was King of the Dwarfs. He carried away beautiful Kunhild and imprisoned her in the Tyrolian Mountains not far from his famous rose garden. The garden was surrounded by a silken thread and guarded jealously by Laurin himself, who exacted the left foot and the right hand of any knight who ventured to enter his garden or break off a single flower from its stem.

Kunhild's brother Dietrich and his friend Dietlieb and companions set out to rescue the fair Kunhild:

> *"Wittich, the mighty champion, trod the roses to the ground,*
> *Broke down the gates, and ravaged the garden far renowned;*
> *Gone was the portal's splendor, by the heroes bold destroyed;*
> *The fragrance of the flowers was past, and all the garden's pride."*
>
> HELDENBUCH (WEBER'S tr.)

The knights fought desperately with Laurin's giants and dwarfs and finally were victorious. Laurin was taken prisoner and to gain his freedom, promised to forswear all his malicious propensities and spend the remainder of his life doing good.

Laurin persuaded the gentle Kunhild to marry him, so the King of Dwarfs and his new Queen went to live in the underground palace in the beautiful rose garden. Peasants and simple-hearted Alpine hunters have often seen the garden but worldly wise and sceptical people have always sought it in vain.

The Rose Garden at Worms Flush with his victory in one rose garden, the knight Dietrich was encouraged to try his skill at the Rose Garden at Worms, on the Rhine, owned by a Burgundian princess. The prize of the victor was a rose garland and a kiss from the princess. Again the knights were successful although one of the company, Ilsan, the monk, cared little for the lovely wreath. He carried his reward of roses back to the monastery, where he pressed it down upon the monks bald pates, laughing aloud when he saw them wince as the sharp thorns pierced them.

Greek Legend

According to Greek mythological legend, Chloris, the deity of flowers, one cloudy morning walked through the woods and found the body of a beautiful nymph. Saddened to see such a lovely creature dead she decided to give her new life by transforming her into a beautiful flower surpassing all others in charm and beauty. She called on the other deities to help her with her task: Aphrodite, to give beauty; the three Graces, to bestow brilliance, joy and charm; her husband, Zephyrus, the West-wind, to blow away the clouds so that Apollo, the Sun, could send his blessing though his rays; and Dionysius, the deity of wine, to give nectar and fragrance.

When the new flower was finished, the gods rejoiced over its charming beauty and delicate scent. Chloris collected a diadem of dewdrops and crowned the new flower, the rose, as the queen of all flowers. Aphrodite presented the rose to her son, Eros, the deity of love. The white rose became the symbol of charm and innocence, and the red rose of love and desire.

When Eros in turn gave the rose to Harpocrates, the deity of silence, to induce him to conceal the weaknesses of the gods, the rose became the emblem of silence and secrecy. In ancient times a rose was attached to the ceiling of council chambers as an indication that everybody present was sworn to secrecy, SUB ROSA—under the rose. The rosette sometimes decorating the centre of the ceiling of our rooms today is an unconscious use of this ancient symbol of secrecy.

Do It Yourself with Roses

Enhancing Literature with the Scent of Roses

"Dry roses put to the nose to smell do comfort
the brayne and the herte and quickeneth the spyryte."
R. BANCKES, 'A little Herball', 1525

There is an intimate link between smell and the automatic nervous system. The Indian doctor Radmajieff, echoed Hypocrates when he said; "odiferous molecules can influence a persons emotions, mental state and philosophy. The way of life is through the essential oils of plants."

In A History of Scents, author Roy Genders quotes a Doctor McKenzie as saying: "of all the senses, none is as mysterious as smell. The nature of the emanations that stir it to activity is still unknown; its effects upon the psyche are both wide and deep, at once obvious and subtle." Genders also quotes Yehudi Menuhin, the great violinist, as saying that he considers scent to be more elusive than music, stirring one's subconcious thoughts and emotions.

Scented Notepaper Send some poetry to a loved one on rose-scented notepaper. Two easy methods of scenting the paper are:
1. Store several sheets of paper in a box with a liberal sprinkling of dried rose potpourri.
2. Saturate a cotton ball with rose essential oil. Remove stationery from box and make holes in the platform in the box in which the stationery comes. Put the cotton ball under the platform. Put stationery back and close box.

Notepaper with a crinkled effect can be achieved by spraying on rosewater with a fine hand spray, and then hanging the sheets to dry in the sun before storing.

Dried Rose Petal Bookmark

Mark the pages of your books with roses by making dried petal bookmarks.

Sheet of colored construction paper
Sheet of laminating film (available from a hobby shop or art supply store)
Piece of rose ribbon or cord
Water-soluble opaque white glue (that dries clear)
Dried rose petals and leaves

Cut construction paper 1 1/2 inches by 7 inches. Glue on petals and leaves in a pretty spray. Cut two pieces laminating film 1 1/2 inches by 7 inches. Fasten one piece over the flowers, the other over the back.

Punch a hole at the top and loop ribbon or cord through. Scent the ribbon or cord by washing in rosewater or in rose extract or by dabbing with rose essential oil.

Rose Filled Bookmark

Cut the shape of the bookmark out of buckram or any other suitable material. Sew together three sides and put rose petals inside. Embroider as needed to make it look nice.

14

Music & Dance

Today the rose reigns supreme as the Queen of Flowers, the title bestowed on it by the Greek poetess Sappho. The earliest known description of the rose was given in an ode written by the Greek poet Anacreon; "when the sea created the beautiful, dew-sparkling Venus . . . the earth, in its part, gave birth to this lovely planet, a new masterpiece of nature . . majestic on her thorny column, this immortal flower".

Roses lent their legendary romance to the Garden of Eden, to the hanging Gardens of Babylon and to the gardens of ancient Persia where nightingales sang and the clove-like scent of damask roses filled the air. This bird of song is depicted in a rose-bordered 18th Century Persian miniature, the nightingale perched on the stem of an outsized damask rose.

As the flower of Aphrodite and the flower of Venus, so in the odes of poets and lays of balladeers, the rose stands for womanly perfection and the mysteries of love.

The rose is also represented in our churches in the form of song. Traditionally a thornless rose is the symbol of the Virgin Mary. An English hymn of the 13th Century says:

> *Lady, flower of alle thing*
> *Rosa sine spina*
> *Thou bere Jhesu, heven King*
> *Gratia divina.*

Popular Songs

There are hundreds of rose songs. One of the most recent is the 1988 smash hit, '18 Wheels and a Dozen Roses', recorded by Kathy Mattea. With this 'rose' single she was the first female artist to top the country charts for two consecutive weeks since Dolly Patron in 1979.

Country music is also represented by Country Road. Their 'Rose Garden' album takes its name from the Lynn Anderson hit of the same name and also includes the song 'Room Full of Roses'.

Another popular album today, 'Roses in Sunshine' by Nana Mouskouri, contains two rose songs.

Should you choose to collect rose records, you might start with the following old favorites:

- Red Roses for a Blue Lady
  (recorded by the Guy Lombardo orchestra)
- Rose of Tralee and Moonlight and Roses
  (recorded by the Irish tenor, John McCormack)
- Rose Marie
  (Jeannette McDonald and Nelson Eddy sang it in the movie)
- Give Me One Dozen Roses and Bouquet of Roses
  (by Sammy Kaye and his orchestra)
- The Yellow Rose of Texas
  (there are two songs with this title, one sung by Mitch Miller and the lesser known melody sung by Roy Rogers)
- I Never Promised You a Rose Garden
- Days of Wine and Roses
- Everything's Coming Up Roses
  (Ethel Merman in 1959 in 'Gypsy' told all of New York)
- One Rose (from The Desert Song)
- Rose Room (recorded by the Jack Hylton orchestra)
- Rose of Washington Square
- My Wild Irish Rose (composed and sung by Chauncey Olcott)
- The Rose (from the movie, sung by Bette Midler)
- Roses of Picardy (sung by Richard Tauber)
- The Last Rose of Summer
  (sung by coloratura soprano, Amelita Galli-Curci)
- Mexicali Rose (sung by crooner Bing Crosby)
- Honeysuckle Rose (by Fats Waller)
- Paper Roses (recorded by Marie Osmond)

- La Vie en Rose
Even Groucho Marx sang 'Give Me a Rose'.

Blooming Star

In August 1989, pop singer, La Toya Jackson (older sister of pop star Michael Jackson), who used to travel with her pet boa constrictor, adopted a new exotic trademark—black roses. In August, La Toya flew to the Soviet Union with dozens of black buds to perform a benefit concert for Moscow's Children's Fund. At that time her latest hit song was Bad Girl; she said she hoped the Soviets would accept her music—not to mention her flowers.

Rose Operas

THE ROSE OF CASTILE: by Michel William Balfe, with a libretto by Harris and Falconer, first performed at London on October 29, 1857.

THE ROSE OF PERSIA: A comic opera in 2 acts by Sir Arthur Sullivan (of Gilbert and Sullivan fame), with a libretto by Basil Hood, first performed at the London Savoy Theatre on November 29, 1899.

DER ROSENKAVALIER: (The Rose Bearer or Cavalier of the Rose)
By Richard Strauss, Libretto by Hugo von Hofmannsthal

Subtitled 'A Comedy for Music', the opera Der Rosenkavalier, has delighted audiences since its premiere performance in Dresden in 1911. It has been performed oftener than any other modern German opera.

The pompous, vulgar and womanizing Baron Ochs tells the Marshallin, Princess von Werdenberg, that he will be calling on his fiance, Sophie. First, however, he must observe the traditional custom of sending a messenger to his bride-to-be with a silver rose as a pledge of his love. The Marshallin suggests that her young lover, Count Octavian, be the messenger.

Octavian arrives at Sophie's home dressed in a glittering costume of white and silver. In his hand he holds the silver rose.

For a moment Sophie and Octavian, each enchanted by the others beauty, stand motionless looking at each other. Then follows the ceremony of the 'Presentation of the Rose'. The exquisite theme of the rose is played upon strings, flutes, harps, and celesta as Octavian says he is bringing a token of love on behalf of his kinsman, the Baron Ochs. Sophie smells the rose and marvels at its wonderful scent. Octavian explains that a few drops of Persian perfume have been poured upon it. Gazing into each others eyes, the two sing that this moment of mysterious enchantment will last throughout eternity.

After the usual confusions of opera, the final scene has the lovers united. Their voices soar to the high notes of the opera's climax and Octavian gathers Sophie in his arms to the theme of the silver rose.

There are many fine recordings of this opera but Sikora's Classical Records in Vancouver, B.C. considers the best one to be the 1957 Angel recording now released on compact disk: Angel CD with the Philharmonia Orchestra under the direction of von Karajan with Elizabeth Schwartzkof, Christa Ludwig and Teresa Stich-Randall.

Dance

LE SPECTRE DE LA ROSE: The rose comes alive in 'Le Spectre de la Rose', created for the great dancer Nijinsky by Fokine and staged by Diaghilev. It was the first great ballet solo for a male dancer. In it Nijinsky plays the Rose Spirit who flies through the window of a young girl who has fallen asleep with the rose from her first ball next to her cheek. Leon Bakst designed the costume. It was made of hundreds of silk petals sewn to a transparent base and covered Nijinsky's body with shifting iridescent pinks like Tiffany glass.

LA ROSE MALADE: The ballet 'La Rose Malade' inspired by William Blake was created for Maya Plisetskaya of the Bolshoi Ballet. The costumes were created by Yves St. Laurent, choreography by Roland Petit and music by Gustav Mahler.

THE SLEEPING BEAUTY: During the second act of 'The Sleeping Beauty', Aurora and her four brothers dance a beautiful Rose Adagio. Each suitor gives Aurora two roses as symbols of eternal love, which Aurora hands teasingly to her mother.

15

Visual Arts

Two of the most ardent devotees of the rose were Cleopatra and the Empress Josephine Bonaparte. Cleopatra wooed Mark Antony amid a bed of roses, while Josephine was the celebrated possessor of one of history's greatest rose gardens at Chateau Malmaison.

No paintings have come down to us of Cleopatra, but Josephine has been depicted in a 19th Century engraving wearing a coronet of pale roses. And, in 'La Rose de la Malmaison,' French artist Jean-Louis Vigier portrays Emperor Napoleon offering Josephine a rose as she sits in her garden with her relatives and ladies in waiting.

At the time of Josephine's death in 1814 she had collected some 250 types of roses many of which live on through a series of paintings by Pierre-Joseph Redoute.

The rose has also become a floral symbol of Christianity. Although shunned by early Christians, who linked it with the excesses of pagan Rome, by the Middle Ages it had undergone a transformation becoming a symbol of the purity of the Virgin Mary. This symbolic association is emphasized in a 15th Century painting 'Madonna and Child in the Rose Garden' ascribed to the Italian artist Stefano da Verona.

Painters

Pierre Joseph Redoute

Pierre Joseph Redoute is the most renowned painter of roses. He was born in Belgium into a family of painters. His family was appalled when he insisted on painting flowers rather than the portraits and battle scenes that provided an income for the family. He was influenced by Dutch flower painters such as Jan van Huysum. His talent was eventually recognized by his patron and lifelong friend, botanist Charles Louis L'Heritier de Brutelle.

Redoute always dreamed of producing a volume of all the roses but it wasn't until the Empress Josephine Bonaparte engaged him to paint the flowers in her garden at Malmaison that he realized the dream. Roses were Josephine's favorite but she died before she could see the finished volume of 'Les Roses', completed in 1824. It features 167 color plates of roses from all over the world from the classical period, the Middle Ages, and the early 19th Century.

Few illustrators since have approached Redoute's ability to render the anatomical details accurately while at the same time capturing the beauty of the rose's color and form in an almost magical way. His botanical drawings are still used today to illustrate books on roses and other flowering plants; his classic roses became for years the standard by which other florals were judged.

His prints and posters are enjoying a resurgence today.

The Ariel Press in London published, in 1954 and 1956, a pair of folio-sized volumes that reproduce four dozen of the Redoute plates, under the titles of 'Pierre-Joseph Redoute Roses 1 and 2', with the original French text.

Paintings

Roses are the dominant flowers in old and new paintings. Portrait, landscape and floral artists all included roses in their compositions. For the rose lover, each new painting discovery is a delight.

The earliest known portrait of a rose, believed to be 4000 years old, is that discovered on a wall near the Palace of Knossos in Crete. This rose has been identified as the so-called Holy Rose, which has been found in Egyptian tombs on a number of occasions and is the 'rosa sancta' described by Richard in his Flora of Abyssinia (1848).

Old Masters

Current garden varieties of R. centifolia, the hundred-leaved or cabbage rose, are so often depicted in the floral art of Dutch masters and in the work of Redoute, that one of the varieties is called 'Rose des Peintres' and another variety is called 'Prolifera de Redoute'.

The old cabbage rose of Provence, *R. centifolia*, evolved by the Dutch breeders during the 17th Century, was widely copied by the Dutch artist Jan van Huysum and later by the French painter, Fantin Latour. Indeed a variety named after the famous French artist may still be obtained. Robust, it is six feet tall and almost as wide. Its graceful, arching branches are covered with large, cup-shaped blooms of a lovely shade of shell pink to make this a most beautiful rose, loved by the painters.

'Flower Still Life' was painted by the Dutch master Jan Davidsz de Heem about 1665 and includes roses in a bouquet. It can be seen at the Ashmolean Museum, Oxford. What gives this picture such appeal is not only the rich variety of shapes and colors but the Baroque energy and vitality of every flower.

'Madame de Pompadour', painted by Francois Boucher about 1755, hangs in the National Galleries of Scotland, Edinburgh. Boucher shows the favorite of Louis XI reposing amidst a gorgeous array of textures— silk, lace, brocade, flowers (including roses) both real and artificial—to set off her powdered beauty.

'Flora', a painting by Titian, hangs in the Uffize at Florence. It is a portrait of a woman, half undraped, with loosened hair, and flowers in her hand. In Roman mythology, Flora is the Goddess of Flowers.

Felix Laurine's painting of a 15th Century floral court hangs in the Academy of Floral Games (of 1948) headquarters in Toulouse, France. It depicts a tournament of troubadors competing before Clemence Isaure, traditional founder of the Academy. One bard, plucking his harp, stands ready to receive a golden rose.

Cecil Golding painted 'Jenny Lind' holding a pink rose with roses in her hair.

'Women in the Garden' by French impressionist, Claude Monet, was painted about 1866 and hangs in the Louvre, Paris. The charming figures in the rose garden have their laps and arms filled with multi-colored roses. Monet's 'Spring Flowers' (1864) shows white roses fresh from picking scattered on a table.

'Mischief' by George Frederick Watts (1817–1904) is in the National Gallery of Scotland and shows a nude couple enmeshed in a tangle of rose briars. Says Watts of his painting: "A symbolical design representing the tyranny of Earthly Love. A stalwart figure typifying the pride and strength of Physical Manhood has been ensnared by passion in the Love and is now fast held amid tangled briars, where he thought to find only roses. Cupid's arrow has struck low, and lies half buried in the earth at his feet." (A classical legend says that when Venus ran through a rose hedge to meet the wounded Adonis, her blood stained the flowers for all eternity).

Modern Paintings

'Island Roses' by Jamie Wyeth includes a huge bush of old roses on a stormy hillside of Monhegan Island, Maine, U.S.A. Although Wyeth is better known for his portraits and studies of people, pigs, pumpkins or bales of hay, even he could succumb to the lure of the rose.

In 'Weeping Rose' drawn by Tretchikoff, the famous White Russian from South Africa, the rose has fallen from its vase and two tears have fallen from the petals: "Another symbol of the sensitivity of flowers. The tears of the rose have fallen in two distinct drops of melancholy at its estrangement from nature and its death in exile." The painting is in the collection of Mr. E.W. Krige.

'Roses' by Peter Ellenshaw is a magical, mystical English garden focusing on a white rose bush with the roses in new bud and at every stage up to full-blown. Ellenshaw utilizes jewel-like colors with just the hint of a cottage in the background. "Every few months, I feel the need to go back to painting my favourite flower—the rose. It is always a delight to me." A signed and numbered reproduction has been produced by Mill Pond Press entitled 'Autumn Roses'.

Reproduction Catalogues

The New York Graphic Society has been a leading publisher of fine art for over 60 years. The lavish, full color catalogue makes a great 'browse'. Ask at your local art gallery or print shop to see a catalogue or the reproductions themselves.

Rose painting reproductions in this or other catalogues include such works as:

'Pink and White Roses' (1890) by Vincent van Gogh, painted two years after his famous 'Sunflowers'. The original is in a private collection.

'Roses' (1879) by Pierre Auguste Renoir is an example of the exquisite floral paintings of this eminent painter. The original painting of a jug of deep pink roses and a single yellow is in a private collection.

(1614-1904)
Jan van Huysum, (Dutch)   Juan de Arellano (Spanish)
Henri Fantin-Latour (French)

(1932-1972)
Raoul Dufy (French)   Andre Derain (French)
Kees van Dongen (Dutch)   Huldah (American)
Armando Miravalls Bove (Spanish)

Piet Mondrian (Dutch, 1872-1944) is best known for his starkly modern lines and primary colored spaces. However, in 1922 he painted two uniquely beautiful blue rose works entitled 'Rose in Tumbler' and 'Blue Rose'

Reproductions of rose designs in various colors by Scherer are available from Art in Motion distributors, Burnaby, B.C. The vibrantly colored renditions of roses are intricately enhanced by the addition of gold foil.

Canadian Art Prints produces a series of work by Lynn Gertenbach. These romantic reproductions depict beautiful ladies in period costume in garden settings or in drawing rooms with Victorian bouquets of roses.

Other reproductions available by contemporary American artists include:
'The Veranda' (1985) by Candace Whittemore Lovely, featuring pink and red rose bushes.
'Harbour Roses' (1981) by Ray Ellis, with white roses over a fence by the sea.
'Tea Roses' (1987) by P.J. Steadman

Oriental 'rose' art is represented by Yun Shou-p'ing, 'Roses and Iris' and Hui Chi Mau, 'Cherry Blossoms and Wild Roses'.

Art of India

'Woman with Rose' is a brush drawing of about 1875 from Kalighat, Calcutta, and depicts a nude holding a single rose.

Do It Yourself with Roses

Painting a Rose

There are many kinds of roses and their structures can differ greatly, but if you can learn to paint one rose well, you can paint any other kind.

Making distinction between petal and petal is essential and needs practice to acquire. Start to paint the flower from the petals in the centre which are usually brighter in shade than any other petals. Try to vary the shades of different petals so as to bring out the third dimension.

In painting a rose or any other flower, first determine the over-all linear rhythm of its design. In the case of the rose this is created by a series of sheets (Fig. 1) describing a spiral rhythm around a central cone (Fig. 2). As the sheets rotate, some of them will fold back or become 'dog eared' (Fig. 3). The complete flower (Fig. 6) then, is composed of circling sheets, 'dog ears', and spiral lines (Figs. 4 and 5).

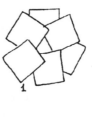

The importance of basic geometric shapes of objects cannot be overemphasized—especially when drawing and painting flowers and leaves. For the rose the square is the geometric base for its lines and shape.

There are many books on easy ways to paint flowers which are found in art supply stores. Or join your local art club or Community College art classes.

Rose Windows

Rose patterns appeared increasingly in church architecture, and most spectacularly in the huge circular rose windows of Gothic cathedrals; these windows are the largest representation of the rose. Beginning in the 12th Century the Gothic cathedrals were built as monuments to faith, the beauty of their stained glass windows defying the darkness of life such as the great plagues and endless wars.

Radiating brilliant sections of color and changing with light outside, the rose windows were ornamented by figures to resemble a rose or a rosette. Their radiating patterns indicated many paths to one centre—this corresponding to the paths that lead to the real self at the centre of the soul.

France is considered the home of the Gothic cathedral. But the arrival of the rose window is somewhat of a mystery. They appeared quite suddenly around the year 1200 and within 50 years had diffused right across France. A few appeared in England, Italy, Spain and Germany, but they remained essentially a French phenomenon and it is around Paris we find the greatest gems. The wheel at Saint-Denis is thought by many to be the first rose.

Although contemporary with Gothic architecture, the rose window's parent was the wheel window of Romanesque architecture. Before evolving into a full blown rose, the wheel developed some wondrous variations and elaborations including wheels within wheels. With the advent of the Gothic style in Paris, a metamorphosis occurred; the wheel became a flower. The term wheel continued long after this transition and the two forms often co-exist in the same window as at Chartres where the west rose is externally a massive wheel but internally has metamorphosed into a perfect flower.

The immediate predecessor of the rose is thought to be the Wheel of Fortune, which in the Middle Ages, symbolized Fate. Its metamorphosis into the rose symbolized the deliverance from Fate—the birth of Christ in the human soul. A rose window at Saint-Beauvais is an example of the Wheel of Fortune evolving into the rose of life.

Each rose window is a symbol of love, the elements and the universe, but it is also a construction that embodies geometry, numbers and light; also there are components of the Logos.

To unite the finite with the infinite through the square and the circle is an aspiration common to Christian and Islamic symbolism, which is embodied in a number of rose windows.

Light, to the medieval mind was a magical substance which contained the power to transform the soul.

Color, light and the sun often play strange tricks on the eye. Red, in the great west rose at Reims, strongly predominates when the sun is out, and at sunset becomes a consuming ball of fire evoking the End of Time.

Geometry and number combine with light and color in the classic north window at Chartres—the 'Rose de France'. Its defined geometry is among its finest glories, everything generated from the properties of the square within the circle. The window is constructed through the number and geometry Fibonacci Series which underlies the growth of many flowers.

Chartres Cathedral

The great rose windows of Paris and Chartres take your breath away with their spectacular webs of glass, lead and stone.

Each of the rose windows at Chartres is a triumph of geometry.

On the west facade of Chartres and facing the setting sun is the great rose of Chartres, 44 feet in diameter; externally a giant wheel and internally a beautiful rose—a masterpiece of light geometry.

A New Testament subject is placed next to one from the Old at Chartres where the north rose with kings, priests and prophets faces the south rose filled with 24 elders of the Apocalypse.

Notre Dame de Paris

The universe is manifested in the form of every rose window, their concentric layers echoing the spheres containing the sun, moon, planets and stars.

In the west rose of Notre Dame de Paris the 'spheres' contain the zodiac, time, the vices and virtues and the prophets, all surrounding the Virgin Mary. The creative 'order' is embodied in numbers, 12 being the number of perfection, of the cosmos and of Christ.

In the south rose at Paris, tinted light glows through the stained glass petals in the shape of a rose which radiate from a central figure of Christ. God was originally surrounded by 4 Evangelists, the 12 Apostles and 24 martyrs or confessors; now, entirely rebuilt twice, the window contains only a few of the original figures.

Notre-Dame de Mantes

The window on the west facade of Notre-Dame de Mantes is the first real rose, breaking away from the strictly spoked structure of the wheel. The subject is the Last Judgment, strongly reminiscent of the west rose at Chartres, with Christ at the centre surrounded on the innermost centre by angels in adoration and by the Virgin Mary and St. John on the left and right of Christ.

Winchester Castle

The Round Table in the wall of the Great Hall at Winchester Castle is strikingly reminiscent of an archetypal rose window. Painted in Tudor times, it has 25 divisions, with Arthur at the top and a Tudor rose at the centre.

Westminster Abbey

The North Transept contains a rose window above the Triforium. The figures of 16 Apostles and Evangelists were designed by Sir James Thornhill in 1721 and it was from his canvases that the glass painter worked. Thornhill's fee was 100 pounds and Joshua Price, the glass painter, received 44 pounds 16 shillings.

This work was done at the time when Sir Christopher Wren and Nicholas Hawksmoor were restoring the north front and designing the new towers at the west end of the Abbey. The stone tracery of the rose window was again remodelled towards the end of the 19th century when the old glass was cleaned and put back again.

Lancing College Chapel

Completed in 1977, this rose window is the largest in England, a position formerly held by Old Saint Pauls burnt in 1666. Nearly 36 feet in diameter, it has over 2500 pieces of glass.

York Minster

The marigold of York Minster, with its red and white roses interwoven into the twelve petals, commemorates the union of the Houses of York and Lancaster by Henry the VII's marriage.

Washington Cathedral, USA

Of all modern rose windows, that of Washington Cathedral is probably the finest. Built Gothic style, using original methods, it contains three traditional rose windows which exploit to the fullest modern glass techniques. The west window, abstract in design and picking up all available light, evokes the Creation: "Let there be light".

Milan Cathedral

In Italy, where the Gothic style of architecture was reluctantly admitted, the most 'French' cathedral is that of Milan, built in the 15th Century. The almost Flamboyant rose in the apse has an interlocking, wavy, flame-like tracery of mouchettes—whence the name Flamboyant.

16

Rose Gardens of the World

During the peak years of the Roman Empire rose cultivation reached its zenith in the ancient world. Universally the nobility and the rich had private rose gardens while the populace enjoyed public rose gardens.

During the 12th and 13th centuries, warriors returning from the crusades in the middle east brought back tales of the magnificent rose gardens as well as sample roses.

In the late 18th century, two important sets of circumstances led to the explosion in popularity of roses that continues to this day. The first was the introduction to the west of roses from China in 1752; they attracted many followers. In contrast to most roses, the China rose bloomed over a period of many months. Just about every modern rose can trace its ancestry to one of these imports.

The second circumstance was the rose garden created at Chateau Malmaison by the Empress Josephine of France. She bought this property three years after her marriage to Napoleon. Here she made continual improvements on the picturesque landscape, in the style of an English park that surrounded the strikingly severe dwelling. And so she created a world-famous rose garden of all known varieties, some 250.

Famous Rose Gardens

Because it is the world's most loved flower, every country has wonderful rose gardens. The following examples may pique your curiosity enough to send you in search of others. Hundreds of North American municipalities are justifiably proud of their rose gardens.

Canada

There are many impressive rose gardens in Canada. Some stand alone; others are contained within variety gardens. Among them are:

UBC BOTANICAL GARDEN
University of British Columbia, 6501 N.W. Marine Drive,
Vancouver, B.C. V6T 1W5
Phone: (604) 228-3928

Wednesdays at 1 pm the Friends of the Garden give tours. The last Sundays of May, June, July and September feature guided tours and tea.

The University of British Columbia Botanical Garden is on Point Grey in Vancouver, B.C. The Rose Garden is at its best in June when more than 2,000 roses are in brilliant bloom.

Take a tunnel underneath Marine Drive to the David Lam Asian garden (Mr. Lam was appointed Lieutenant Governor of British Columbia in 1988). Set in a natural coastal forest, this 30 acre garden includes Asian roses.

THE BUTCHART GARDENS
Box 4010, Stn A, Victoria, B.C. V8X 3X4
Phone: (604) 652-4422 or 652-5256 for 24-hour recorded information.
Open year round from 9 am every day.

In 1904, the concept of The Butchart Gardens began as an effort to beautify a worked-out quarry site on the 130-acre estate of Mr. and Mrs. R.P. Butchart, pioneers in the manufacture of Portland Cement in Canada. Their hobby became a family commitment to horticulture and hospitality spanning more than eighty years and delighting visitors from all over the world. From the charming English Rose Garden to the exquisite Sunken Garden, this 50-acre showplace today maintains the gracious traditions of the past in one of the loveliest corners of the world.

June through September the entire Gardens and Ross Fountain are magically illuminated by thousands of hidden lights and at nightfall on Saturdays during July and August, the sky explodes with fireworks.

STANLEY PARK

Vancouver, B.C.

The rose garden is situated within the beauty of a 1000 acre forest park in the heart of downtown Vancouver.

QUEEN ELIZABETH PARK

33rd Avenue and Cambie Street, Vancouver, B.C.

Atop Little Mountain, two former stone quarries have been transformed into two beautiful sunken gardens. A flower lover's delight, it also houses the Bloedel Conservatory, a triodetic dome filled with tropical plants.

PARK AND TILFORD GARDEN

North Vancouver, B.C.

These gardens were developed by the Park and Tilford Company on the grounds of their distillery. The site is now next to The Bridge movie production studio facility in North Vancouver. The six gardens feature year-round displays: rose, rhododendron, colonnade, native wood and oriental.

VAN DUSEN BOTANICAL GARDEN

5251 Oak St., Vancouver, B.C. V6M 4H1

Phone: (604) 266-7194

Created from 55 rolling acres of golf course, this botanical garden includes a rose garden.

MINTER GARDENS

52892 Bunker Road, Rosedale, B.C.

Phone: (604) 794-7191

Hours of operation are: April through October, daily from 9 am to dusk. Minter Gardens is located 75 miles east of Vancouver on the Trans-Canada Highway #1 at the exit to world famous Harrison Hot Springs. The ten theme gardens include a traditional Rose Garden, Hanging Basket Bower and Fern Garden.

LARKWHISTLE

Near Miller Lake, Ontario

Larkwhistle is an extraordinary garden near Miller Lake, Ontario, where author Patrick Lima and photographer John Scanlon enjoy the truly unusual pleasure of living entirely from their plants—selling herbs, giving tours and photographing and describing what they grow. At Larkwhistle dozens of old-fashioned roses share space with more than 150 kinds of herbs.

For three weeks to a month, always in early July after the peonies are finished, the old roses billow with bloom. Most flower once very generously but some give a small encore in the fall. They have perfumes lost in most newer hybrids.

Other Canadian Botanical Gardens to Visit

ARBORETUM, OTTAWA
   Research Station, Research Branch, Agriculture Canada,
   Ottawa, Ontario K1A 0C6
   Phone: (613) 995-9827

ASSINIBOINE PARK
   2355 Corydon Ave., Winnipeg, Manitoba R3P 0R5
   Phone: (204) 885-1500

CALGARY BOTANICAL GARDENS
   St. George's Island, Box 3036, Stn. B, Calgary, Alberta T2M 4R8
   Phone: (403) 265-9310

DEVONIAN BOTANIC GARDEN of the University of Alberta
   Edmonton, Alberta T6G 2E9
   Phone: (403) 987-3054

HUMBER COLLEGE ARBORETUM
   205 Humber College Blvd., Rexdale, Ontario M9W 5L7
   Phone: (416) 675-3111, extension 4445/4113

THE MEMORIAL UNIVERSITY BOTANICAL GARDEN
   at Oxen Pond, Memorial University of Newfoundland
   St. John's, Newfoundland A1C 5S7
   Phone: (709) 737-8590

MONTREAL BOTANICAL GARDEN
4101 E. Sherbrooke St., Montreal, Quebec H1X 2B2
Phone: (514) 252-1173

MORGAN ARBORETUM
Box 500, Macdonald College, Ste-Anne-de-Bellevue
Quebec H9X 1C0
Phone: (514) 457-2000

ROYAL BOTANICAL GARDENS
Box 399, Hamilton, Ontario L8N 3H8
Phone: (416) 527-1158

UNIVERSITY OF GUELPH ARBORETUM
Guelph, Ontario N1G 2W1
Phone: (519) 824-4120

The prairie provinces of Canada are very active in the research and development of hardy strains based on shrub roses rather than the more delicate hybrid teas. Morden, Manitoba, has developed a widely recognized series of roses.

United States
REINICH ROSE GARDEN
Gage Park, Topeka, Kansas

At the time of its construction in 1931, Reinich was one of the largest municipally owned rose gardens in the United States. Covering some 10 acres in Gage Park, it still retains its international fame as one of the finest all-round collections.

Some 300 varieties of climbers, floribunda, polyantha, hybrid perpetual and tea rose grow and thrive. There is a dazzling abundance of more than 7000 rose bushes. The fragrant rectangular beds are set about a lily-filled central pool. In an adjoining Rose test garden, many of the roses grow for two years before being put on the commercial market.

Surrounding the central part of the rose garden, 25 beds of roses outline the history of the rose. One of the first among the ancient traditional flowers is *Rosa gallica officinalis*, the 'Apothecary' rose, that flourished in Europe before it was brought to America. This rose is the ancestor of today's hybrid perpetuals.

TULSA MUNICIPAL ROSE GARDEN
Woodward Park, Tulsa, Oklahoma

This municipal, terraced rose garden began in 1934 at a meeting of the Tulsa Garden Club. Today it is a remarkable collection of new and old rose varieties. Among the 9000 roses is 'Mr. Lincoln' — huge, fragrant, perfect for cutting.

The upper terrace, at the top of a gentle incline, falls gradually in five other terraces to street level some 900 feet below. Along the east side of the highest terrace are trellises filled with climbing roses, among them 'Charlotte Armstrong, Chevy Chase, Tiffany, Chrysler Imperial, Royal Gold' and 'Bloomfield Courage'. They augment a display that includes 'Dainty Bess', often known as the queen of single roses, an orchid-pink rose with large soft petals.

The second terrace includes such beauties as the magnificent grandiflora, 'Queen Elizabeth' with its huge soft-pink flowers; the 1940 All-American rose selection, 'Worlds Fair'; and the beautiful 'Soeur Therese' that was introduced by French rose breeders in 1930.

On the third terrace is a sampling of the roses of Sam McGredy, a famous rose breeder, and on the fourth and fifth terraces are roses of more recent origin, among them the clear pink floribunda, 'Gene Boerner', and the brilliant orange red, double-blooming grandiflora, 'Comanche'.

THE HERSHEY ROSE GARDENS AND ARBORETUM
A famous public rose garden in the Lebanon Valley,
Hershey, Pennsylvania.

In April 1936, Milton S. Hershey, 'the chocolate king', was invited to a conference dinner where he was asked for a contribution of $1M to help establish a national rosarium. Mr. Hershey proposed instead to establish a rose garden at Hershey.

Work started almost immediately on a three-and-a-half acre plot just south of Hotel Hershey. By late August the garden was ready for fall planting and by early November more than 1200 roses in 112 varieties had been set out. The garden was opened to the public in May of 1937.

Mr. Hershey was so pleased with the public interest that the garden was enlarged. In 1937, 7000 roses were added and the following year, 4000 more. Today this is one of the finest rose gardens to be found. In the acres of terraced beds there are 4200 rose bushes in 1200 varieties in every shade and color.

England
MOTTISFONT ABBEY
Near Winchester, England

The Abbey is home for a collection of historical roses on the site of a 12th century monastery. The roses — a full half acre of them—exhale a wave of sweetness that is the very essence of rose.

THE GARDENS OF THE ROSE
St. Albans, Herts, England

The Gardens of the Rose is the home and showpiece for The Royal National Rose Society in England. The Gardens contain one of the most important collections of roses in the world—superbly grown and beautifully displayed.

The 12 acres of grounds provide the visitor with a delightful and unforgettable display of over 30,000 rose plants—a living catalogue of roses past and present. And, for the real enthusiast, there are also the Trial Grounds where roses come for trial from many countries of the world.

The Gardens are open from early June to the end of September but the peak of perfection is in early July when the huge plantings of Modern Large Flowered (Hybrid Tea) and Cluster Flowered (Floribunda) varieties are in the full flush of their first flowering.

In 1955, Fred Fairbrother suggested that the Royal National Society consider a suitable property on the north side of London. A long search eventually led, in 1959, to Bone Hill with its large and delightful brick country house and eight acres of gardens — four acres were added later.

The Gardens include plantings which integrate herbaceous plants and early-flowering Species and Old Garden roses, which are of great interest in early June. Among them are Damasks and Gallicas, Centifolieas, Albas and Portlands. Perhaps attracting the most attention are the lovely bright yellow 'Canary Bird' and the June-flowering *Rosa moyesii* 'Geranium' with its striking crimson-red, single blooms.

The Trial Ground area is bordered with roses which have received awards from the Society. By gracious permission of Her Majesty Queen Elizabeth the Queen Mother, this is known as The Queen Mother's Rose Border.

The main Display Gardens include Hybrid Perpetuals, Bourbons, Rugosas and other kinds, as well as the bed of roses suitable for planting as ground cover, a use which nowadays interests so many garden owners.

Towards the house, the pergola and pool, are massed ranks of modern roses. Near the House is a sunken garden, planted and terraced with Miniature roses.

On the west wall of the Henry Edland Memorial Pavilion there is a fine specimen of 'Climbing Iceberg', still considered by rosarians generally as the best pure white Cluster Flowered rose in its bush form.

In the last week of February the gardens are open to Society members and the public for a series of pruning and planting demonstrations.

In June, members are treated to two days of talks and demonstrations by the country's top rose growers and horticulturists. In July, the Society holds its annual spectacular, Britain's Two-Day National Summer Show and Festival which includes the Rose Growers Association annual exhibition.

India

When it is off season in the Northern hemisphere why not visit Indian rose gardens. December to March are the best months as the temperatures are not too high. Among the many famous gardens are:

- Indian Agricultural Research Institute Rose Garden, Pusa, New Delhi.
- National Rose Garden at Chanakyapuri, New Delhi, maintained by The Rose Society of India.
- Zakir Hussain Rose Garden, Chandigarh, Haryana.
- Rose Gardens at Indira Park and Sanjivayya Park, maintained by the Municipal Corporations at Hyderabad.

New Zealand

According to one rose expert, Brian Stretch, of the Canadian federal government Agricultural Research Station in Summerland, B.C., "New Zealand has a climate conducive to growing roses. Every city has wonderful gardens," he said, "but among the most impressive are Wellington Botanical Gardens and Auckland Rose Garden."

Other Wondrous Sites

World's Largest Rose Tree

The 'Lady Banksia' (*Rosa banksiae*), the world's largest rose tree was planted by a Scottish immigrant lady in 1885 in the frontier town, Tombstone, Arizona. The 'Lady' is located in the patio of the Rose Tree Inn Museum at 4th and Toughnut Sts.

The trunk has a circumference of 58 inches and stands over 9 feet high. In full bloom, this tree has over 200,000 white blossoms, enough to easily fill a palace ballroom. Its branches spread out over an arbor covering 5,400 square feet under which 150 people can be comfortably seated. It requires some 68 posts and thousands of feet of iron piping to support it.

The Banksian rose is a rare Chinese climbing species, with small white or fawn-colored flowers of great beauty.

Lime Kiln

At Claydon near Ipswitch, England, grower Humphry Brooke has a rosarium, Lime Kiln, where he grows many Old Roses. There the *moyesii* seedling 'Freia' (Wagner's goddess of perpetual youth) has a diameter of over 48 feet from 32 trunks, immensely prickly for about 7 feet and then smooth to about 30 feet. In autumn it is a waving mass of hips. 'Freia' is pale pink as were all ancient roses.

Rose Associations

Every rose lover should belong to one of the many local, regional and international rose associations. These associations keep you up to date on your favorite flower—the latest varieties, new growing techniques and where rose shows and festivals are being held (there are hundreds). Some associations also put out informative newsletters such as 'The Rose' published by:

THE ROYAL NATIONAL ROSE SOCIETY
Chiswell Green, St. Albans, Herts, AL2 3NR.

You will also hear about available rose tours to famous gardens in many countries, rose competitions and trials, related rose activities such as rose painting and craft exhibitions, rose gifts, etc. Some of the tours may give you access to private gardens not otherwise available to the general public.(See The Gardens of the Rose, p.169).

THE AMERICAN ROSE SOCIETY
Box 30,000, Shreveport, LA 71130.

The American Rose Society boasts more than 20,000 members, mostly amateurs, making it the largest special plant society in the United States. There are more than 350 local chapters and affiliated rose societies throughout the country.

This society has established the American Rose Centre, a 118-acre park planted extensively in roses in Shreveport, Louisiana, which is its headquarters.

It publishes the 'American Rose' magazine monthly as well as the 'American Rose Annual', a hard-bound book sent to its members. It has an extensive lending library and carries out research programs on a cooperative basis at various colleges and experimental stations. Two national rose conventions with meetings and rose shows are held each year.

In its 'Handbook for Selecting Roses', the Society tabulates hundreds of individual reports from all over the country into an annual report of national ratings of all commercially available roses.

THE HERITAGE ROSES GROUP
United States

Northeast:
Lily Shohan
RD 1
Clinton Corners, NY 12514

Southwest:
Miriam Wilkins
925 Galvin Drive
El Cerrito, CA 94530

Northcentral:
Henry Najat, MD
Route 3
Monroe, WI 53566

Southcentral:
Vickie Jackson
122 Bragg Street
New Orleans, LA 70124

Northwest:
Jerry Fellman
947 Broughton Way
Woodburn, OR 97071

Southeast:
Dr. Charles G. Jeremias
2103 Johnstone Street
Newberry, SC 29108

The Heritage Roses Group was formed in 1975 as a fellowship of those who grow and enjoy old roses. A membership list is available for a small fee so you may contact other members in your area. Some areas have sub-groups that meet two or three times a year.

Devotees of old roses formed the group so that they might share their enthusiasm, experiences, and even their roses. For a small annual membership fee you can receive their informative quarterly, 'The Rose Letter'. Send inquiries to Patricia Cole, Drawer K. Mesilla, NM, USA 88046.

THE CANADIAN ROSE SOCIETY
c/o Dianne D. Lask
686 Pharmacy Avenue
Scarborough, Ontario   M1L 3H8

Methods

Drying Roses

Gather roses on a dry morning after the dew is gone and after a rainless period of at least 24 hours. The fresher the flower, the more essential oil remains after the flower dries. Never use roses which have been sprayed with pesticide.

A screen or a piece of cheesecloth suspended between two chairs makes a convenient drying rack. Select an area away from strong light where warm air can circulate. Spread the petals, leaves and buds on the rack. Stir or turn them daily until they are like cereal flakes. This can take from 4 days to 2 weeks.

For moist potpourri, dry the petals for only a few days—until they are limp, not crisp.

If you happen to own a station wagon or other motor vehicle which heats up rapidly on a sunny day, it can be used to get your roses off to a quick drying start. Place the petals on absorbent paper in shallow boxes and place them in the car. Park the car in the shade so the petals won't bleach out. The petals will be almost crisp in one or two days.

Another quick drying method is to place the petals on a cookie sheet and put in a warm oven (110°F) . Leave the oven door open to allow the moisture to escape. Stir or shake from time to time. The drying will take one to two hours.

Store petals in air tight containers and protect them from light. Keep in a cool, dark, dry cupboard for maximum color and aroma.

The strength of dried petals is intensified after moisture is removed. Some cosmeticians believe that the quality of a cream or lotion increases when dried, rather than fresh, flowers (herbs, fruits and vegetables), are incorporated into the product and rubbed into moistened skin.

Equipment for Rose Recipes

When making rose recipes you will need the following basic equipment. Many items will already be in your kitchen. Thoroughly wash equipment whenever preparing a new batch. To get good uncontaminated products, you must keep everything clean.

1. Bowls, saucepans, double boiler, measuring cups, and storage jars. These should be stainless steel, glass, or enamelware (be sure it is not chipped). Never use aluminum. Save all useful jars and bottles but stay away from plastic if you can. Often it is not boilable and some tend to 'leak' oils. Always throw away the insides of the covers.

2. Measuring spoons, electric beater, blender, scales, thermometer (high temperature immersion), strainer, cheesecloth, funnel, filter paper, spatula and wooden spoons or glass stirring rods.
   Whether to strain with a strainer, cheesecloth or use a filter depends on the size of the particles to be removed. Finer more liquid solutions go through a filter readily. Thicker solutions will hardly go through a filter but will go through a strainer or cheesecloth.

3. Eye droppers. Handy for measuring oils and can be bought at the drugstore. When a recipe calls for 'one dropper', this is equivalent to 20 to 24 drops. Generally when adding essential oils the precise number of drops is not critical.

4. Hot plate and large electric frying pan.
   Some recipes call for heating over water. A double boiler will work fine. So will a sturdy heavy baking dish (one that can take direct heat on top of the stove) with two inches or so of water in it. You can also use an electric frying pan half filled with

water. This way you can put two small pots or pyrex cups into the water at once and keep them at the same temperature—very important when making emulsions. A hot plate is helpful if you work away from the kitchen area.

5. Inexpensive decorative labels. You should label everything you make. No matter how good your memory, after awhile one mixture begins to look like another. Put the date on all perishable goods.

6. A notebook. Keep track of all your products. The more information you cram into this book the more you will learn and grow.

Tools for Growing Roses

Gifts for yourself or other rose gardeners. Find them in any good garden supply shop:

Secateurs (pruning shears), pruning saw, rose sucker remover, plant labels, garden twine, gardener's pocket knife, indelible pencil, gardening apron with pouch pocket and kneeling pads, a trug (a shallow basket for carrying flowers, made from strips of wood) for dead heading, gardening gloves, sprayer and watering cans.

Water/Alcohol

Distilled water is preferred wherever water is listed in recipes. It is available at drug stores, garages (where it is called battery water) and supermarkets.

Alcohol: Isopropyl, the familiar rubbing alcohol, is usable for all external applications but not for mouth washes and other preparations taken orally. Ethyl alcohol is suitable for internal use. This is difficult to purchase without a permit but vodka (80% proof) can be substituted.

Preservatives

If you do not want to use chemical preservatives such as methyl paraben, be sure and store short-life preparations in the refrigerator. However, many home-made items will keep indefinitely provided they are put in stoppered bottles or closed containers. Make sure the containers are sterilized.

Suppliers

All materials listed in our formulas can be obtained from botanical and chemical supply houses, herbalist shops, drugstores and supermarkets. Some have mail order arrangements. Check the yellow pages in your phone book.

Herbs, rose petals, rose greeting cards, rose cosmetics and other supplies are also available from: The World of Roses, Sonni Okanagan Enterprises Inc., 43 Van Horne St., Penticton, B.C., Canada V2A 4J9.

If you have the garden space, planting your own rose and herb garden will bring numerous rewards. The methods for drying roses can also be used for herbs.

WEIGHTS AND MEASURES
Apothecaries' Weights
(use apothecary scales)

60 grains	=	1 dram
8 drams	=	1 ounce
12 ounces	=	1 pound
15 1/2 grains	=	1 gram

1. A drachm is a dram, in apothecaries' weight, a unit equal to 60 grains or 1/8 of an ounce.
2. In avoirdupois weight, a dram is a unit equal to 27 1/3 grains or 1/16 of an ounce.

Apothecaries' Liquid Measures

60 mininms or drops	=	1 liquid dram
8 liquid drams	=	1 liquid ounce
16 liquid ounces	=	1 liquid pint
1 1/3 drams	=	1 common teaspoon
3 teaspoons	=	1 tablespoon

Common Measures

60 drops	=	1 teaspoon
3 teaspoons (tsp.)	=	1 tablespoon
2 tablespoons (tbsp.)	=	1 fluid ounce
8 fluid ounces (oz.)	=	1 cup = 16 tbsp.
2 cups	=	1 American pint = 16 fluid oz.
2 pints	=	1 American quart = 32 fluid oz.

Metric Measure

1 gram	=	about 1/28 ounce (.0022046 lb. or 15,4324 grains troy)
1 ounce	=	28.350 grams
1 milliliter (ml.)	=	0.0338 fluid oz.
1 liter (l.)	=	2.1134 liq. pt.
1 liter (l.)	=	1.0567 liq. qt.
1 liter (l.)	=	0.9081 dry qt.
1 liter (l.)	=	0.2642 gal.

1 fl. oz.	=	29.573 ml.
1 liq. pt.	=	0.4732 l.
1 liq. qt	=	0.9463 l.
1 dry qt.	=	1.1012 l.
1 gal.	=	3.7853 l.

Index

'When Nero honoured the house of a Roman noble with his Imperial presence at dinner, there was something more than flowers; the host was put to an enormous expense by having (according to royal custom) all his fountains flinging up rose-water, while the jets were pouring out the fragrant liquid, while rose leaves were on the ground, on the cushions on which the guests lay, hanging in garlands on their brows, and in wreaths around their necks; the couleur de rose pervaded the dinner itself, and a rose-pudding challenged the appetites of the guests.

'To encourage digestion there was rose wine, which Heliogabalus was not only simple enough to drink, but extravagant enough to bath in. He went even further by having the public swimming baths filled with wine of roses and absinthe.

'After breathing, wearing, eating , drinking, lying on, walking over, and sleeping upon roses, it is not wonderful that the unhappy ancient grew sick. His medical man touched his liver and immediately gave him a rose draught. Whatever he ailed, the rose was made in some fashion or other to enter into the remedy for his recovery.

'If the patient died, as he naturally would, then of him more than of any other it might be truly said that he *"died of a rose in aromatic pain"*.'

Translated quotation from 'Memoire sur l'Influence des Odeurs', a famous French work on perfumes.

 Notes

 Notes

 Notes